H. H Lewis

A Gunner Aboard The 'Yankee'

H. H Lewis
A Gunner Aboard The 'Yankee'
ISBN/EAN: 9783744673150
Printed in Europe, USA, Canada, Australia, Japan
Cover: Foto ©ninafisch / pixelio.de

More available books at **www.hansebooks.com**

A GUNNER ABOARD THE "YANKEE."

ACKNOWLEDGEMENT

Acknowledgements are due to J. Harper Skillen, Stewart Flagg, George Yardley, W. G. Wood, and E. Howe Stockwell for the use of photographs; and to C. B. Hayward and Allan H. Seaman for the use of notes and diaries.

THE NAVAL RESERVES LEAVING NEW YORK—GOING OFF IN THE TUGBOAT TO MAN THE "YANKEE" (*page* 8).

A GUNNER ABOARD THE "YANKEE"
FROM THE DIARY OF NUMBER FIVE OF THE AFTER PORT GUN

THE YARN OF THE CRUISE AND FIGHTS OF THE NAVAL RESERVES IN THE SPANISH-AMERICAN WAR

EDITED BY
H. H. LEWIS
LATE U.S.N
WITH
INTRODUCTION
BY
W. T. SAMPSON
REAR ADMIRAL
U.S.N

NEW YORK
DOUBLEDAY & McCLURE CO
1898

Copyright, 1898, by
DOUBLEDAY & McCLURE CO.

EXPLANATION OF TITLE-PAGE

The flags on the title-page indicate the official number of the U. S. S. Yankee, number 592. It is read from the top down, as follows:

The red and white flag is called a "cornet"; it indicates that the flags following it make an official ship's number. The flag below that is the regular Navy code flag five, the next nine, the lowest two.

The long red, white and blue pennant is the commission pennant placed at the topmast head when a vessel goes into commission; there it flies till the ship is formally out of commission.

TO THE NAVAL RESERVE ORGANIZATIONS

THROUGHOUT THE UNITED STATES, WHO HAVE MADE SUCH AN ENVIABLE RECORD DURING THE SPANISH-AMERICAN WAR AND BEFORE WHOM SUCH A GLORIOUS FUTURE OPENS

THIS BOOK IS RESPECTFULLY

DEDICATED

INTRODUCTION.

As the Commander-in-Chief of the American Naval Squadron blockading Santiago and the Cuban coast, the auxiliary cruiser "Yankee," manned by the New York Naval Reserves, came immediately under my observation, and it is a pleasure for me to speak of the spirit and efficiency shown by the officers and crew during their stay under my command.

The young men forming the ship's company of the "Yankee" were called into service several weeks prior to any other Naval Reserve battalion; they came from all walks of civil life, and their minds, devoted to peaceful pursuits, were suddenly diverted to the needs and requirements and the usages of naval routine. Notwithstanding this radical change, they have made the name of their ship a household word throughout the country, and have proved that the average American, whether he be clerk or physician, broker, lawyer, or merchant, can, on the spur of the moment, prove a capable fighter

INTRODUCTION.

for his country even amid such strange and novel surroundings as obtain in the naval service. These young men have especially upheld the American supremacy in the art of gunnery, and have, on all occasions, proved brave and efficient.

The conclusion of the Spanish-American War released them from their voluntarily assumed positions in the regular navy, but when they returned to civil life they carried with them the consciousness of duty well done at Santiago and Cienfuegos and whenever their guns were used in hostile action. In a word, the Naval Reserves manning the "Yankee," in common with those on board other vessels in the service, have proved their aptitude for sea duty, and made apparent the wisdom of the Government in calling them into active service.

W. T. SAMPSON,
Rear-Admiral, U. S. N.

U. S. FLAGSHIP "NEW YORK,"
September 3, 1898.

CONTENTS.

CHAPTER		PAGE
	INTRODUCTION	ix
	PREFACE	1
I.	IN WHICH THE "YANKEE" GOES INTO COMMISSION	4
II.	IN WHICH WE GET UNDER WAY AT LAST .	17
III.	IN WHICH THE "YANKEE" CRUISES FOR PRIZES	30
IV.	WE GET ORDERS TO GO SOUTH .	43
V.	A WILD GOOSE CHASE .	57
VI.	WE BECOME COAL HEAVERS	73
VII.	WE ENTER THE "THEATRE OF WAR" . .	87
VIII.	WE JOIN SAMPSON'S FLEET .	101
IX.	CLEAR SHIP FOR ACTION . . .	115
X.	WE BOMBARD SANTIAGO DE CUBA .	130
XI.	A PERILOUS MOMENT . . .	146
XII.	IN SEARCH OF ADVENTURE . .	161
XIII.	A NARROW ESCAPE . .	176
XIV.	WE ENGAGE IN A SEA FIGHT . .	192

CONTENTS.

Chapter		Page
XV.	Coaling in the Tropics	208
XVI.	"Remember the Fish"	222
XVII.	In God's Country	237
XVIII.	The "Yankee" Arrives off Santiago	254
XIX.	Hope Deferred	269
XX.	Taps	284
	Appendix	297

LIST OF ILLUSTRATIONS.

	FACING PAGE
THE NAVAL RESERVES LEAVING NEW YORK—GOING OFF IN THE TUGBOAT TO MAN THE "YANKEE"	*Frontispiece.*
"THAT FAT MAN IN THE CELLAR WANTS ME TO SLEEP IN A BAG—"	19
"BEGAN TO SCRUB THE JUMPER AS IF IT WAS A FLOOR"	36
"ALL HANDS OF THE WATCH 'TURNED TO' AND SCRUBBED DECKS"	36
"THE 'KID' HAPPENED TO BE NEXT ME WHEN 'STOPPING CLOTHES' ON THE LINE"	38
"THE SIX-POUNDERS ON THE SPAR DECK BEGAN TO BARK"	38
"THE GIG WAS LOWERED"	50
"THE MEN ON THE STAGES"	50
"THE 'YANKEE' DROPPED HER ANCHOR OFF TOMPKINSVILLE"	77
"WITH A FRIGHTFUL ROAR THE DEFECTIVE CARTRIDGE EXPLODED"	82

LIST OF ILLUSTRATIONS.

	FACING PAGE
"Stand by, Men. Be Ready for Instant Action"	100
"The Six-Pounders on the 'Yankee's' Forecastle Joined in the Chorus"	112
"Clear Ship for Action!"	115
The Bombardment of Morro Castle, Santiago	138
On the Gun Deck during the Bombardment	152
The Searchlight "Sweeping Back and Forth Across the Black of the Horizon"	175
"Every Hour a Signal Boy came Running Aft to Read the Log"	185
"All Hands on the Cat Falls!"	185
"There was Temporary Confusion"	203
"Our Appearance Beggared Description"	216
"Took Advantage of the Time to 'Caulk off'"	216
"The Fusillade was Lively"	221
"Saw the Men lying round the Gun in Heaps"	236
"The Decks were Swabbed Thoroughly"	236
"The Spar Deck was Covered with Red Shellac"	240
"The Marines Aired their Hammocks on the Forecastle Deck"	240
"The Blankets and Mattresses were Spread for Airing"	244
"Under the Hose"	244

LIST OF ILLUSTRATIONS.

	FACING PAGE
"He got his Orders from the Bridge"	258
"All You Men who want to go in Swimming may do so"	258
"The 13-inch Charge of Smokeless Powder was Lowered Down"	263
"The Admiral went over in our Gig"	263
"Eight Bells"	289
"Sang out as he Heaved the Lead"	289
Marching through City Hall Park, New York City	295

COLORED PLATES.

Signal Flags showing the "Yankee's" Official Number	Title-page.
Wigwagging and Night-Signalling	90
Official Flags and Pennants	180
The Navy Code of Flag Signals	250

A GUNNER ABOARD THE "YANKEE."

PREFACE.

When the important events of the first part of April, 1898, were shaping themselves toward an inevitable conflict between Spain and the United States of America, the authorities at Washington began to perfect their plans for an immediate increase of the navy. The Naval Militia of the country, of whom Assistant Secretary Theodore Roosevelt had a very high opinion, came in for early attention, and word was sent to the different States to prepare for service. Several days previous to the actual outbreak of war, messages were forwarded from the Naval Reserve receiving ship "New Hampshire," lying at a dock in the East River, to a number of young men, members of the Naval Militia, residing in New York City. These summons contained simply a request to report at once on board the ship, but they resulted in a most curious and interesting transformation—in fact, they formed the foundation of a chain of events which was destined to amalgamate into a common grade—that of a naval bluejacket—several hundred young Americans, who, in their natural characters, were sons of rich men and of men of moderate means, of doctors and lawyers and brokers and clerks and bookkeepers, and of all sorts and conditions of respectable citizens. Patriotism was the incentive which called these youths of various stations together, and sheer love of country and the courage to fight her battles formed the cement which bound them cheerfully to their duty. To fight for pay and as a profession is one thing; to offer your freedom and your life, to endure discomforts and actual hardships, to risk health in a fever-stricken foreign country, and to sacrifice settled ambition for mere patriotism, is another. It is the latter which the Volunteer Naval Reserve of the United States has done, and every American citizen with a drop of honest blood in his veins will surely give the organization the praise it so richly deserves.

On the third of May, while Cervera's whereabouts was still an absorbing mystery, the "Yankee" (an auxiliary cruiser, converted from the steamship "El Norte") went into commission at the Brooklyn Navy Yard. She was manned entirely, save for the captain, executive officer, navigator, paymaster, and the marine guard, by members of the New York State Naval Militia. For four months she remained in commission, weaving the threads of a glorious record which will ever redound to the credit and honor of the Volunteer Naval Reserve. Truth is ever stranger than fiction, and the simple story of the boys of the gallant "Yankee," as set forth in the diary of Number Five of the After Port Gun, should appeal to the heart of every reader in this great country of ours—a country made grander and better and more potent in the world's history by the achievements of such brave lads as those who formed the crew of the "Yankee." Number Five's diary was written simply for his family, but the fame gained by the "Yankee" leads the publishers to believe that it will prove interesting to Americans far and wide. It is set forth in narrative form, but the incidents and the straightforward, simple, and sailor-like words are those of the actual participant. This is his story.

CHAPTER I.

IN WHICH THE "YANKEE" GOES INTO COMMISSION.

U. S. S. "NEW HAMPSHIRE,"
April 26, 1898.

Report at "New Hampshire" immediately, ready to go on board auxiliary cruiser "Yankee."

(Signed)
JOHN H. BARNARD,
Lieut. commanding 3d Division,
N. Y. State Naval Militia.

It was this telegram, brief but extremely comprehensive, received early on the morning of the twenty-sixth of April, which sent me post-haste to the old receiving-ship "New Hampshire," moored at the end of an East River dock. The telegram had been anxiously expected for several days by the members of the First Battalion, and when I reached the ship I found the decks thronged with excited groups.

War was a certainty, and the very air was filled with rumors. The prevailing topic was discussed from every point of view, and within sixty seconds as many destinations had been picked out for the "Yankee." It was variously reported that she was to go to Havana, to Manila, to Porto Rico, and even to Spain. This last rumor brought shouts of laughter, and "Stump," as we termed him, a well-known young insurance broker of New York, remarked, in his characteristic way :

"It probably won't be this particular 'Yankee,' boys, that will go there, but there'll be others."

There was much cleaning of kits and furbishing of cutlasses. We knew that we would not take the latter with us, but then it was practice, and we felt anxious to do something martial as a relief to our excitement. There was a diversion shortly before noon, when the "old man" (the captain) appeared with a number of official-looking papers in his hands.

"He's got the orders," whispered little Potter, our latest recruit. "Whoop! we'll get away this morning, sure."

The whistle of the bosun's mate on watch echoed shrilly about the decks a few moments later.

"Now, d'ye hear there," he shouted, hoarsely, "you will break out mess gear and get yourselves ready for messing aboard ship."

That did not sound as if we were destined to see our new vessel put into commission very soon, and there was some grumbling, but the boys fell to work with good grace, and we were soon preparing for our stay aboard the old frigate. The officer of the deck was lenient, however, and the majority of the crew secured permission to sleep at home that night.

The following Monday, on reporting on board the " New Hampshire," we learned that the entire detail selected to man the " Yankee " would proceed to that ship shortly after eight bells. Word was passed that our enlistment papers—for we were to regularly enter Uncle Sam's naval service—would be made out, and that our freedom and liberty, as some of the boys put it, would cease from that hour. The latter statement made little impression. We had entered the Naval Reserves for business, if business was required, and we expected hardships as well as fun.

A navy-yard tug, sent by the Commandant, steamed alongside at two o'clock, and the company was marched on board without delay. The boys were eager to enter on this, their first real detail, and, in the rush to gain the deck of the tug, young Potter slipped from the rail and fell with a mighty splash into the water. " Man

THE "YANKEE" GOES INTO COMMISSION.

overboard!" bawled his nearest mate, and "Man overboard!" echoed one hundred and fifty voices. There was a scramble for the side, and the tug's deck hand, assisted by several of our fellows, fished Potter from the river with a boat hook.

"Hereafter, please ask permission before you leave the ship," facetiously remarked the officer in charge.

"Humph! as if I meant to do it," grunted Potter, wringing the East River from his duck shirt.

We caught our first view of the "Yankee" as we steamed past the cob dock at the yard. We were favorably impressed at once. She is a fine-looking ship, large, roomy, and comfortable, with lines which show that she is built for speed. As her record is twenty knots an hour, the latter promise is carried out. The "Yankee" was formerly the "El Norte," one of the Morgan Line's crack ships, and, when it was found necessary to increase the navy, she was purchased, together with other vessels of the same company, and ordered converted into an auxiliary cruiser. Gun mounts were placed in the cargo ports, beams strengthened, magazines inserted, and interior arrangements made to accommodate a large crew. The "Yankee's" tonnage is 4,695 tons; length, 408 feet; beam, 48 feet. The battery carried consists of ten five-inch quick-firing breechloaders, six six-pounders, and two Colt automatic guns. After events proved conclusively the efficiency of the "Yankee's" armament.

The detail was taken alongside the "Yankee" by the tug. We had our first meeting with our new captain, Commander W. H. Brownson, of the regular navy. His appearance and his kindly greeting bore out the reputation he holds in the service as a gentleman and a capable officer. It is well to say right here that Commander Brownson, although a strict disciplinarian, was ever fair and just in his treatment of the crew. Our pedigrees were taken for the enlistment papers, and the questions asked us in regard to our ages, occupations, etc., proved that the Government requires the family history of its fighters. The following day each man was subjected to a rigid physical examination. The latter ceremony is so thorough that a man needs to be perfect to have the honor of wearing the blue shirt. Personally, when I finally emerged from the examining room, I felt that my teeth were all wrong, my eyes crossed, my heart a wreck, and that I was not only a physical ruin, but a gibbering idiot as well. That I really passed the examination successfully was no fault of the naval surgeon and his assistants.

After the medical department had finished with us, the enlistment papers were completed, and we became full-fledged "Jackies," as "Stump" termed it. The members of the battalion were rated as landsmen, ordinary seamen, and able-bodied seamen, according to their skill, and a number of men, hastily enlisted for the purpose, were made machinists, firemen, coal-passers, painters, and carpenters. Some of these had seen service in the regular navy, and they were visibly horny-handed sons of toil. One Irishman, whose brogue was painful, looked with something very like contempt on the Naval Reserve sailors.

"Uncle Sam is a queer bird," several of us overheard him remark to a mate. "He do be making a picnic av this war wid his pleasure boats an' his crew av pretty b'yes. If we iver tackle the Spaniards, there'll be many a mama's baby on board this hooker cryin' for home, swate home."

"Hod," a six-footer, who played quarter-back on a famous team not long ago, took out his note-book and made an entry.

"I'll spot that fellow and make him eat his words before we get into deep water," he said, quietly. He was not the only one to make that vow, and it was plain that Burke, the Irishman, had trouble in store for him.

On our return to the "New Hampshire," the battalion was placed under the regular ship's routine. All the men were divided into two watches, starboard and port. The port watch, for instance, goes on duty at eight bells in the morning, stands four hours, and is then relieved by the starboard watch; this routine continues day and night, except from four until eight in the afternoon, when occur the dog watches, two of them, two hours long each, stood by the port and starboard men respectively. The dog watches are necessary to secure a change in the hours of duty for each watch.

From now on we were given a taste of the actual work of the service. Details were made up each morning and sent to the "Yankee" to assist in getting her in readiness for service. One of the first duties was to carry on board and stow away in the hold one hundred kegs of mess pork. As each keg contained one hundred pounds, the task was not easy for men unaccustomed to manual labor. Still there was no complaint. In fact, the only growling heard so far had come from some of the men who had seen service in the regular navy. Burke, the fireman, de-

THE "YANKEE" GOES INTO COMMISSION.

claimed loudly against the "shoe leather an' de terrer-cotter hard-tack which they do be tryin' to feed to honest workers. As for the slops they call coffee, Oi wouldn't give it to an Orangeman's pig!"

The food served out on board the "New Hampshire"—being the usual Government ration of salt-horse, coffee, and hard-tack—was vastly different from that to which the majority of the boys were accustomed, but it was accepted with the good grace displayed by the members of the Reserve on every occasion. All these little discomforts are, as the Navigator (a commissioned officer of the regular navy) remarked, "merely incidental to the service."

As the time approached when we were to board the "Yankee" for good, the ordinary watches were abandoned, and only anchor watches kept. An anchor watch is a detail of five or six men, selected from the different parts of the ship, who do duty, really, as watchmen, during the night. Two days before the order arrived to leave the "New Hampshire," it was found necessary to station several men, armed with guns and fixed bayonets, on the dock near the ship, to stop men from taking the "hawser route" ashore. The firemen and coal-passers had been refused shore leave, or liberty, as it is called, because of their habit of getting intoxicated, pawning their uniforms, and loitering ashore. Truth to tell, the guns and bayonets had little effect, as the offenders were old in the business.

The second night after the order was put in force it happened that "Hod," who was rated as an able seaman, was on duty with gun and bayonet on that end of the dock opposite the forecastle. He had just relieved the man whose watch ended at midnight, and he stood thoughtfully watching the twinkling lights on the opposite side of the mighty East River. There was so much to occupy his mind in a situation which was both charming and fascinating that he remained motionless for several minutes. Presently there came a slight, scraping sound, and the end of a rope struck the dock almost at his feet.

Glancing up, "Hod" saw a man's figure, dimly outlined in the gloom, slip from the topgallant forecastle and quickly descend the rope. It was evidently one of the men taking "French" leave, and it was the sentry's duty to give the alarm at once. But "Hod" had other views in this particular case. Hastily stepping back into the shadows, he laid his gun upon the floor of the dock, and rolled up his sleeves with

THE "YANKEE" GOES INTO COMMISSION.

an air that meant business. The next moment the absconder dropped from the rope.

As he prepared to slip past the ship a sinewy hand was placed upon his shoulder, and another equally sinewy caught him by the collar.

"Burke, suppose you return aboard ship," said "Hod," quietly. "You are not going to hit the Bowery this time."

The Irish fireman attempted to wrench himself free, then he struck out at "Hod" with all the force of his right arm. The quarter-back's practice on the field came into play, and the college graduate tackled his opponent in the latest approved style. The struggle was short and decisive, and it resulted in Burke declaring his willingness to return to the ship.

"The next time you try to size up a new shipmate be sure you are on to his curves," remarked "Hod," as he escorted his prisoner over the gangway. "You will find some of 'mama's pretty boys' rather tough nuts to crack."

The day following this little episode found the members of the State Naval Militia detailed to form the crew of the "Yankee" in full possession of the cruiser which they were to sail to glory or defeat in defense of their country. The ship's company, two hundred and twenty-five in all, boarded the auxiliary warship without ceremony, and were speedily set to work hoisting in provisions, removing to the yard all unnecessary stuff with which the ship was littered, and getting her generally in condition for sailing. The work was extremely hard, but it was done without demur.

A naval officer attached to the yard stood near me at one time during the afternoon, and I heard him remark to a visitor who had accompanied him on board : " You will find an object lesson in this scene. These young men working here at the hardest kind of manual labor, buckling down cheerfully to dirty jobs, were, a few days ago, living in luxury in the best homes in New York City. The older men were clerks, or lawyers, or physicians, and not one of them had ever stained his hands with toil. Look at them now."

Unconsciously I glanced across the deck to where three men were hauling upon a whip, or block-and-tackle, which was being used to hoist huge boxes and casks of provisions on board. The three men were working sturdily, and it would have been difficult to recognize in them, with their grimy faces and soiled duck uniforms, a doctor, a bank cashier, and a man-about-town well known in New York City. Near the forward hatch, industriously swabbing the deck, was a black-haired youth whose father helps to control some of the largest moves on 'Change. Scattered about the gangway were others, some painting, some rolling barrels, and a number engaged in whipping in heavy boxes of ammunition. They were all cheerful, and the decks resounded with merry chatter and whistling and song.

I turned to myself. My hands were brown and smeared and bruised. My uniform, once white, was streaked and stained with tar. I wore shoes innocent of blacking and made after a pattern much admired among navvies. I had an individual ache in every bone of my body, and I was hungry and was compelled to look forward to a dinner of odorous salt-horse, hard bread, and "ennuied" coffee, but I was happy—I had to admit that. Perhaps it was the novelty of the situation, perhaps it was something else, but the fact remained that I would not have left the ship or given up the idea of going on the cruise for a good deal.

We worked hard all day, and, when mess gear was piped for supper, we could hardly repress a sigh of heartfelt relief. The food, bad as it was, was welcome, and when I reluctantly swung away from the mess table I felt much better. At six bells, shortly before hammocks were piped down, the "striker," or helper, for our mess cook, said mysteriously :

"Don't turn in early, Russ, there's going to be a little fun. 'Bill' and 'Stump' have young Potter on a string. It will be great."

CHAPTER II.

IN WHICH WE GET UNDER WAY AT LAST.

The hint of possible fun that night was sufficient to keep me alert. "All work and no play, etc.," was part of our code aboard the "Yankee," and goodness knows we had worked hard enough getting the ship ready for sailing to be permitted a little sport. Then, again, any badgering of young Potter would be innocent amusement, so I laid by and waited, keeping my eye on "Bill."

"Bill," by the way, was the captain of our mess, a jolly good fellow, popular, and always in evidence when there was any skylarking on foot.

Hammocks were piped down at seven bells (7:30 p.m.), and, as it was our first experience on board the "Yankee," there was some confusion. A number of new recruits had joined that afternoon, and their efforts to master the mysteries of the sailor's sleeping outfit were amusing. A naval hammock differs largely from those used ashore. A hammock aboard ship is of canvas, seven feet long, with holes a few inches apart at each end, through which are reeved pieces of strong cord. The latter are called clews, and they meet at an iron ring, which is attached to the hooks in the carline beams when the hammock is in position for use. When a hammock is properly slung it hangs almost straight, with very little sagging. To get in properly, one grasps two hoops near the head, and, with an agile spring, throws body and feet into the canvas bed. This requires a knack, and is learned only after a more or less painful experience. A three-inch mattress and two blankets go with each outfit. For sheets a bag-like mattress cover is used, and, in lieu of the downy pillows of home, the sailor must be content with his shoes rolled up inside his trousers or flannel shirt. With it all, however, the naval hammock is very comfortable. There is the advantage of being able to not only wash your blankets and sheets, but your bed as well. Once each month clean hammocks are issued and the old ones scrubbed.

While I was below, rigging up my clews, I saw a commotion on the other side of the deck. The master-at-arms was expostulating with one of the new recruits who had reported that afternoon. Suddenly the latter called out, angrily, " I'll see

"THAT FAT MAN IN THE CELLAR WANTS ME TO SLEEP IN A BAG—"
(*page* 19).

if I have to, durn you!" and bolted for the upper deck. The master-at-arms followed him at once, and several of us followed the master-at-arms to see the excitement. We reached the quarter-deck just as the recruit came to a stop in front of the officer on watch.

"What's the matter with you?" demanded the latter, curtly. "What's up?"

"Th-th-that m-m-man down in the—the cellar wants me to sleep in a bag, durn him," gasped the recruit, waving his lanky arms, "and I won't do it for him or no one else."

"Cellar?" Then the officer shouted with laughter.

The recruit was sent back to the "New Hampshire" next day, but it was long before the master-at-arms was known by any other name or title than "the man in the cellar."

A few minutes before tattoo, "Bill" and "Stump" came up and intimated by signs that I was to accompany them to the forward part of the berth deck. On reaching the extreme end, which was occupied by an immense hawser reel, "Bill" indicated a hammock which was swinging with the forward clews directly above the great spool, or reel.

"If young Potter doesn't think this old hooker is haunted I'll never play another joke," he chuckled. "Get in and show him, 'Stump.'"

The latter grasped two hooks, gave himself a swing, landed in the hammock, and in an instant struck the deck with a thump, the hammock under him. As he rolled out I rubbed my eyes. The hammock had swiftly returned to its former position!

"It isn't hoodooed," grinned "Bill." "Just look here."

He hauled up on the head clews and presently a five-inch shell appeared above the top of the reel. The shell was fastened to the end of the hammock lashing, at the other end of which was attached the ring. The lashing led over the hook, and the weight of the shell was just sufficient to keep the hammock in its place. As I finished inspecting the clever contrivance, the boatswain's mate piped tattoo.

We hurried away to watch from a distance. Laughing and singing, the fellows trooped down to prepare for turning in; the hard labor of the day had not dampened their spirits. The deck soon presented an animated scene. A number of us had slept long enough on board the "New Hampshire" to become accustomed to man-o'-war style, but the new recruits were like so many cats in a strange garret. They stood about,

WE GET UNDER WAY AT LAST.

glancing doubtfully at their hammocks and then at their clothes. They did not know just what to do with either.

"How do you get into the thing, I wonder?" asked the fellow from Harlem, eyeing his suspended bed.

"Borrow the navigator's step-ladder," suggested the coxs'n of the gig. "He keeps it in the chart room."

The greatest difficulty was the disposal of our clothes. There were no wardrobes nor closets nor convenient hooks, and it was strictly against the rule to leave anything lying around decks. The question was solved presently by an old naval sailor, who calmly made a neat roll of his duck jumper and trousers and another of his shoes and shirt. The latter he tucked into his clews at the foot, and the other he used as a pillow. We thanked our lucky stars we did not have creased trousers, smooth coats, vests, white shirts, collars, and neckties to dispose of.

In due time young Potter, who had stayed on deck viewing the scenery until chased by the corporal of the guard, came down and made for his hammock. Four dozen pairs of eyes watched him with delightful anticipation. Unconscious of the attention he was attracting, he doffed his clothes and brought out something from his black bag which proved to be a night-shirt! If there was any compunction in regard to the trick intended for him, it instantly vanished. A sailor with a night-shirt was legitimate prey.

Whistling softly, the victim prepared himself for the swing, grasped the hooks, and then, with good momentum, landed in the hammock. There was a swish, a distinct thud, and young Potter rolled out upon the deck with a gasp of amazement. Turning as quickly as he could, he looked up and saw the hammock swinging in its proper place. It was physical labor for us to keep from howling with glee at the expression on his face. He glanced sheepishly about to see if his catastrophe had been observed; then he made another attempt. This time a heave of the ship sent him even more quickly to the deck, and he landed with a bump that could have been heard in the cabin. He was fighting mad when he again scrambled to his feet.

"I can lick the lubber who threw me out," he shouted.

"Stop that talking," came from the master-at-arms' corner. "Turn in and keep quiet about the decks."

Potter grumbled something under his breath, then he made a careful search in the vicinity of his hammock. It was worth a dollar admission to see him poke about with the end of a broom. He found nothing suspicious, and proceeded to try again. Very gingerly he grasped the hooks, and he experimented with one foot before trusting his whole weight to the hammock. The second he released his hold of the hooks he fell, and the fall was even greater than before.

"The blamed thing is spooky!" he howled, as he gathered himself together. He made a quick run for the ladder leading on deck, but was stopped by the master-at-arms, who demanded an explanation. While they were arguing, "Bill" and I quickly fixed the hammock, casting off the shell and concealing it behind a black bag. We had barely finished when the chief petty officer came up and examined the clews. He tested them by applying his own weight, then gave the crestfallen and astounded Potter a few terse words of advice about eating too much supper. Five minutes later the deck was quiet.

The hard labor of the previous day—such labor as hauling and pulling, handling heavy boxes and casks, and bales and barrels of provisions and ammunition—had made me dead tired, and I slept like a log until reveille. This unpleasant function occurred at three bells (half-past five o'clock), and it consisted of an infernal hubbub of drums and bugles and boatswains' pipes, loud and discordant enough to awaken the seven sleepers. We roused in a hurry, and, with eyes scarcely open, began to lash up our hammocks.

"Seven turns, no more, no less," bawled the master-at-arms. "Get just seven turns of the lashing around your hammocks, and get 'em quick. If you can't pass your hammock through a foot ring, you'll go on the report. Shake a leg there!"

The rumor had gone about that it was the custom to "swat" the last man with a club, and there was a great scramble. We found the hammock stowers in the nettings, which were large boxes on the gun deck, and our queer canvas beds were soon stowed away for the day. As the reveille hour is too early for breakfast, coffee and hard-tack is served out by each mess cook. The coffee is minus milk, but it is hot and palatable, and really acts as a tonic.

The first order of the day is to scrub down decks and clean ship generally, but, as the "Yankee" was still in the throes of preparation, we were spared that disagreeable work and permitted to arrange our belongings for the long voyage before us. In the service each man is allowed a black bag about three feet six inches high and twelve inches in diameter, and a small wooden box, eighteen inches square, known as a "ditty box," to keep his wardrobe in. All clothing is rolled, and careful sailors generally wrap each garment in a piece of muslin before consigning it to the black bag. In the ditty box are kept such articles as toothbrush, brush and comb, small hand glass, writing material, and odds and ends. Each bag and box is numbered, and must be kept in a certain place. At first we thought it wouldn't be possible to keep our clothing in such a small space, but experience taught us that we would have ample room.

The following days until the eighth of May were days of manual labor, which hardened our muscles and placed a fine edge on our appetites. To see the men who had been accustomed to a life of luxury toiling away with rope and scrubbing brush and paint pot, working like day laborers, and happy at that, was really a remarkable spectacle. For my part, I noticed with surprise that scratched and bruised hands—scratched so that the salt water caused positive pain—did not appeal to me. I tore off a corner of my right thumb trying to squeeze a large box through the forward hatch, and the only treatment I gave it was a fragment of rather soiled rag and a little vaseline borrowed from a mate.

To quit work and apply for the first aid to injured never struck me. Ashore I would probably have called a doctor.

The day before we left the yard one of my mates sprained his back lifting a box of canned meat. In civil life he had been a lawyer with a promising practice, his office being with one of the best known men of the bar. He gave it up and joined the Naval Reserves because, as he expressed it, "To fight for one's country is a patriot's first duty." When the accident happened, he refused to go below to the sick bay until the doctor stated that rest for a few days at least was absolutely necessary.

"It isn't that I mind the hurt, boys," he said, with a smile, as he was assisted to the hatch, "but I hate to be knocked out in my first engagement, and that with a box of canned corned beef."

The monotony of work was broken on the ninth of May, when preparations were made to leave the yard. The destination was only Tompkinsville, but there was not a man on board but felt that, as the last hawser was cast off, we were fairly started on our cruise in search of action. As the "Yankee" was assisted away from the wharf by a Government tug, a number of friends gathered ashore cheered lustily and waved their hats and handkerchiefs. The scene had been repeated time without end, no doubt, but it went to our hearts all the same, and there was many a husky note in the cheers we gave in return.

There was also encouragement in the whistles we received as we dropped down the East River, and we felt as if our small share in the war would be appreciated by those compelled to stay at home. We steamed directly to the vicinity of Fort Wadsworth, Staten Island, anchored off Tompkinsville, and then picked up a berth there for the night. Half way down the bay we met a tug carrying a committee from the "Sons of the Revolution" of New York State. The committee had been selected by the society to present us with a set of colors. The tug accompanied us to our anchorage, then the committee came on board. The ceremony of presentation was rather picturesque.

The visitors gathered on the bridge, the ship's bugler sounded the assembly, and in obedience to the call we lined up on the forward deck. We wore the white duck service uniform, including trousers, jumper, and cap. Some of the uniforms had suffered in contact with pitch, but the general effect was good. When everything was in readiness, the chairman of the committee presented the set of colors and said :

"Captain Brownson, officers and men of the 'Yankee,' I have the honor, on behalf of the Society of the Sons of the Revolution in the State of New York, to present these colors to the members of the Naval Reserve of the State of New York, who have enlisted for service under your command."

He continued by hoping that the colors would ever float victorious, and said that he did not doubt it, and then our skipper made a little speech in reply. The affair wound up with a round of cheers and general congratulations. The flags were handsome, and, as it came to pass, they flaunted amid battle smoke before many weeks.

Our stay off Tompkinsville was to be short, but we had time to become acquainted with a characteristic naval oddity known as the bumboat. Diligent inquiries among the old sailors on board the "Yankee" failed to enlighten me as to the derivation of the name, but the consensus of opinion was that these floating peddlers sold articles which, to use a slang phrase, were pretty "bum." Experience has given the opinion some color of truth. Our bumboat boarded us early and stayed with us until the corporal of the guard called "time."

She came laden with pies and doughnuts, pins

and needles, tape and buttons and whisk brooms and shoe blacking, handkerchiefs, ties, scissors, soap, writing paper, envelopes, ink, pens, cakes, bread, jelly, pocket knives, and a schedule of prices that would have brought a blush of envy to the face of a Swiss inn-keeper. As the boys had not yet grown entirely accustomed to what is called "Government straight," i.e., salt meat and hard-tack, the bumboat did a thriving business. Young Potter's bill was tremendous, and Mrs. Bumboat bade him a regretful farewell when she visited us for the last time.

At three in the afternoon of the tenth we hoisted anchor on our way to sea. Our good friends had not deserted us, and a number of them, aboard several tugs, accompanied us as far as the Narrows. The "God-speed" given us as we steamed away would have been a fine object lesson to our future antagonists.

Up to the present we had been concerned simply with the preparations for war, but it was destined that before another twenty-four hours had passed we would have a taste of the actual realities.

The "Yankee" was to see service.

CHAPTER III.

IN WHICH THE "YANKEE" CRUISES FOR PRIZES.

It was evening, the evening of the day on which the "Yankee" sailed from Tompkinsville bound out on her maiden cruise as an auxiliary ship of war. The afternoon had passed without event, save that which attacks the amateur sailor when he first feels the heaving swell of old ocean. The crew had shaken into its place, and the men of the watch on deck were commencing to appreciate their responsibilities.

The ship was quiet, save for the faint chug-chug of the propeller under the stern and the occasional clang of a shovel in the fire room deep down in the innermost reaches of the ship. The sun had vanished in a hazy cloud which portended a stiff breeze, but the wind was still gentle, and, as it swept across the decks from off the port quarter, it seemed grateful indeed to those who came from below for a breath of air.

Orders had been issued to darken the decks. The running lights of red and green were still in the lamp room, and, except for a soft, rosy glow from the binnacle-bowl, there was a blackness of night throughout the upper part of the ship. Cigars and pipes and cigarettes had been tabooed, and doors were opened in the deck houses only after the inside lights had been lowered to a flickering pin point.

Up on the forward bridge Captain Brownson stood talking in a low voice to the executive officer, Lieutenant Hubbard. The lurching swing of the ship caused them to sway back and forth against the rail and a metallic sound came from a sword scabbard suspended from the captain's belt. The presence of this sword, betrayed by the clatter it made, told a secret to several sailors gathered under the lee of the pilot house, and one said, in an excited whisper:

"There's something up, Chips. The old man is fixed for trouble. I'm going aft and stand by."

The speaker started off, but before he had taken ten steps the shrill blast of a bugle suddenly broke the stillness of the night. The discordant notes rang and echoed through the ship, and, while the sound was still trembling in the air, two score of shadowy figures sprang up from different parts of the deck and scurried toward the ladders leading below.

The transformation was instant and complete.

From a ship stealthily pursuing its way through the darkness—a part of the mist—the "Yankee" became the theatre of a scene of the most intense activity.

There was no shouting, no great clamor of sound ; nothing but the peculiar shuffling of shoes against iron, the hard panting of hurrying men, the grating of breech-blocks, low muttered orders from officer to man, and a multitude of minor noises that seemed strange and weird and uncanny in this blackness.

A belated wardroom boy, still carrying a towel across his arm, slips from the cabin and hastens forward to his station in the powder division. The navigator, an officer of the regular navy, whose ideas of discipline are based on cast iron rules, espies the laggard and administers a sharp rebuke. A squad of marines dash from the "barracks" below and line up at the secondary battery guns on the forecastle. Some of the marines are hatless and coatless, and one wiry little private shambles along on one foot. He stumbles against a hatch-coaming and kicks his shoe across the deck.

Suddenly an order comes out of the gloom near the main hatch and is carried from gun to gun.

"Cast loose and provide!"

The hitherto motionless figures waiting at the battery spring into activity. Hands move nimbly at the training and elevating gear. Breech-blocks are thrown open, sights adjusted, the first and second captains take their places, the former with the firing lanyard in readiness for use at his gun; then there is silence again as the officer in charge of the division holds up one hand as a signal that all is prepared. Then comes the word to load.

In a twinkling the ammunition hoists are creaking with their burdens and boxes of shell appear on deck. These are quickly lifted to the guns and taken in hand by the loaders. The latter do their part of the general work thoroughly and with despatch, and presently the breech-blocks are swung to and the battery is ready for action.

In the meantime there has been systematic preparation in other parts of the auxiliary cruiser. Down in the sick bay aft, the surgeon and his assistants have made ready for their grewsome task. Cases of glittering instruments have been opened, lint and bandages and splints are in their proper places, and the apothecary and bayman are getting the cots in trim for instant use.

In the fire room the firemen and coal-passers are heaping up the furnaces, a couple of men hurry away to attend to the fire mains, and, standing by in readiness for duty, are the engineers and crew of the off watch. The carpenters are ready below with shot-hole plugs, and everywhere throughout the ship can be found officers and sailors and marines and men of the "black gang," each at his proper station in readiness for the word to begin action.

But that word does not come. Instead a stentorian command is heard from the bridge:

"Secure!"

Laughing and joking, the crew of the "Yankee" hasten to restore the ship to its former state. All this has been a drill, the drill known as general quarters. It is the first time it has been held under service conditions, and when the captain steps down from the bridge and says in his brisk, authoritative way, "Very well done, very well done indeed," the boys of the cruiser are satisfied and happy.

Twice during the night the drill is repeated. There is no grumbling because of disturbed sleep, for a rumor has gone about the ship that Spanish vessels have been seen off the coast, and even the cranks on board admit that drills and exercises are necessary.

THE "YANKEE" CRUISES FOR PRIZES.

Sea watches have been set, and the rules followed when under way are now operative. A brief explanation of the routine attending the first hours of a naval day may help to make succeeding descriptions more plain. The ship's daily life commences with the calling of the ship's cook at 3:30 a.m. The ordinary mess cooks are awakened at four o'clock, so that coffee can be prepared for the watch. Coffee is always served with hard-tack to the watch coming on deck at four. It is all the men get until breakfast at 7:30, and a great deal of work must be accomplished before that time.

After the hard-tack and coffee had been consumed—and it went to that spot always reserved for good things—the lookouts of the other watch on the port and starboard bridge and the patent life buoys port and starboard quarter were relieved. As soon as the first streaks of dawn were to be seen a long-drawn boatswain's pipe, like the wail of a lost soul, came from forward, and the order "scrub and wash clothes" given.

A day or two before the "Yankee" left the navy yard, one of the pretty girls who had come over to visit her asked: "Where do you have your washing done? It must require a great many washerwomen to keep the clothes of this dirty [glancing rather disdainfully at her somewhat grimy friend] crew clean." Though we knew that the luxury of a laundry would not fall to our lot, we were at a loss as to the method pursued to clean clothes.

We soon learned.

We who had been anticipating an order of this sort came running forward with bundles of clothes that would discourage a steam laundry. This was the first opportunity we had had to clean up. The forecastlemen led out the hose, which was connected to the ship's pump, and, after wetting down the forecastle deck (where all clothes must be scrubbed), we were told we might turn to.

The "Kid," who was the youngest member of the crew aboard, very popular with officers and men, and who afterward became the ship's mascot, said, "How do you work this, anyway?" I confessed that I was in the dark myself, but proposed that we watch "Patt," the gunner's mate, who had served in the navy before. Presently we saw him lay his jumper flat on the deck, wet it thoroughly with water from the hose, then rub it with salt-water soap. Then he fished out a stiff scrubbing brush and began to scrub the jumper as if it was a floor. We then understood the significance of the order *scrub* and

"BEGAN TO SCRUB THE JUMPER AS IF IT WAS A FLOOR" (*page* 36).

"ALL HANDS OF THE WATCH 'TURNED TO' AND SCRUBBED DECKS" (*page* 39).

wash clothes. In salt water the clothes have not only to be washed, but scrubbed as well.

The "Kid" remarked, "Well, I'll be switched," and forthwith fell on his knees and proceeded to follow "Patt's" example.

Though we scrubbed manfully, "putting our backs into it" and "using plenty of elbow grease," as instructed, still the result was hardly up to our expectations. The navigator remarked, as we were "stopping" the clothes on the line, "You heroes might scrub those clothes a little bit; it does not take a college education to learn how to wash clothes."

I agreed with the "Kid" that, though cleanliness was next to Godliness, cleanliness, like Godliness, was often a difficult virtue to acquire. We found it almost impossible to be cleanly without the aid of fresh water, so the schemes devised to avoid the executive's order and get it were many and ingenious.

One man would go to the ship's galley, where the fresh water hand-pump was, and, without further ado, begin to fill his bucket, remarking, if the cook attempted to interfere, that he had to scrub paint work or he had orders from the doctor to bathe in fresh water. These excuses would be successful till too many men came in with buckets and plausible excuses, when the cook would shut down on the scheme for the time. The man with fresh water was the envy of his fellows, and must needs be vigilant, or bucket and water would disappear mysteriously.

The "Kid" happened to be next me when "stopping" his clothes on the line, and remarked, as he tied the last knot on his last jumper, "I like to be clean as the next chap, but this scrubbing clothes on your knees is no snap."

He stopped to feel them.

"Why, I can feel the corns growing on them already. How often do we have to do this scrubbing job, anyhow?" he asked.

"You *can* do it every morning, if you really feel inclined," I replied, smiling at his rueful countenance; "clothes can only be washed during the morning watch (four to eight), I understand, and, as the starboard men are on duty one day during that time and the port watch the next, each is supposed to 'scrub and wash clothes' in their own watch. See?"

The "Kid" looked up at the dripping line of rather dingy clothes, then down at his red and soapy knees, and said, as he turned to go aft, "Well, when we get back to New York, I am going to have a suit of whites made of celluloid that can be washed with a sponge."

At 6:30 the order "knock off scrubbing

"THE 'KID' HAPPENED TO BE NEXT ME WHEN 'STOPPING' CLOTHES ON THE LINE" (*page* 38).

"THE SIX-POUNDERS ON THE SPAR DECK BEGAN TO BARK" (*page* 47).

clothes" was given, and then all hands of the watch "turned to" and scrubbed decks, scoured the gratings and companion-way ladders with sand and canvas, brass work was polished, paint work wiped down, and everything on board made as spick and span as a new dollar.

A vast quantity of water is brought from over the side through the ship's pump, and the men work in their bare feet. In fact, the usual costume during this period of the day consists of a pair of duck trousers and a thin shirt. On special occasions even the shirt is dispensed with. During warm weather it is delightful to splash around a water-soaked deck, but there are mornings when a biting wind comes from the north, and the keenness of winter is in the air, and then Jackie, compelled to labor up to his knees in water, casts longing glances toward the glow of the galley fire, and makes his semi-yearly vow that he will leave the "blooming" service for good and go on a farm.

This scrubbing of decks and scouring of ladders put an extra edge on our appetites, so we agreed with "Stump" when he said, "I feel as if I could put a whole bumboat load of stuff out of commission all by my lonely." "Stump's" appetite was out of proportion to his size.

When the boatswain's mate gave his peculiar long, quavering pipe and the order " spread mess gear for the watch below," at 7:20, we of the watch on deck realized that there was still forty minutes to wait. Every man's hunger seemed to increase tenfold, so that even the odor of boiling " salt-horse " from the galley did not trouble us.

Finally the order came, " on deck all the starboard watch "; followed by the boatswain's mess call for the watch on deck. The scramble to get below and to work with knife, fork, and spoon resembled a fire panic at a theatre. It is first come first served aboard ship, and the man who lingers often gets left.

The gun deck of the " Yankee," like the gun deck of most war vessels, is Jack's living room. Here he sleeps, in what he facetiously calls his folding-bed, which is swung from the deck beams above; here he enjoys the various amusements that an ordinary citizen would call work; here he goes through his drills; here he fights, not his shipmates, but his country's enemies, and here he eats.

The remark, " he spread his legs luxuriously under the mahogany," would hardly apply to Jack's mode of dining. His table is a swinging affair that is hung on the hammock hooks—a mere board a couple of feet wide and twelve or fourteen feet long, having a ridge around the edge to keep the plates from sliding off in a seaway. Jack's dining chairs are called "mess benches," and consist of a long folding bench that with the table can be stowed away in racks overhead when not in use. A mess chest for each mess, an enamelled iron plate and cup, and a knife, fork, and spoon for each man complete the "mess gear" outfit.

The ship's company is divided into messes, each man being assigned to a certain mess at the same time his billet number or ship's number is given to him. There are from fifteen to thirty men in a mess. Each has its own "berth-deck cook," who prepares the food for the galley; each, too, has a mess caterer, or striker, whose business it is to help the mess cook and see that all goes well. The caterer is a volunteer from the mess, and generally serves for a week, when another volunteer takes his place. If the quantity or quality of the food is not up to expectations, it would be better for the caterer that he be put down in the "brig" out of harm's way, for Jack is apt to speak his mind in vigorous English, and his mind and stomach have generally formed a close alliance.

The twenty minutes allowed for meals are

well spent, and the clatter of knives and forks attests the zest with which Uncle Sam's man-o'-war's-man tackles his not always too nice or delicate fare. The nine dollars a month allowed by the navy for rations is expended by the paymaster of the vessel, not by the men, so, if the paymaster concludes that the men shall have "salt-horse," rice, and hard-tack, Jack gets "salt-horse," rice, and hard-tack, and that is all he does get unless his mess cook and caterer are unusually prudent and save something from the previous day's rations, or the mess has put up some extra money and has " private stores."

As the man with the biggest appetite or the fellow who eats slowly are putting away the last morsel of cracker hash or the last swallow of coffee, " Jimmy Legs " (the master-at-arms) comes around, shouting as he goes, " Shake a leg there, we want to get this deck cleared for quarters." He is often followed by the boatswain's mate of the watch, who echoes his call, and between them they clear the deck. Then begins the real work of the day.

CHAPTER IV.

WE GET ORDERS TO GO SOUTH.

Shortly after breakfast the "Yankee" came to anchor outside of Provincetown, Mass. An hour later a large man-of-war was discovered steaming toward us. Rumors were rife at once, and the excitement increased when the vessel, which proved to be the gallant cruiser "Columbia," passed close alongside, and the captain was observed to lean over the bridge railing with a megaphone in his hands.

"'Yankee' ahoy!" came across the water.

"Hello, 'Columbia!'" replied Captain Brownson.

"I have orders for you."

"Whoop! we are going to Cuba," cried young Potter. "It's dead sure this time. They can't do without us down——"

"Silence!" called out the executive officer, sternly. "Corporal of the guard, see to that man."

Poor Potter is sent below in disgrace amid the

chuckles and jeers of his unsympathetic shipmates. The little episode nearly earned him many hours of extra duty.

In the meantime the "Columbia's" captain had communicated the welcome intelligence that we were to cruise to the southward at once to look for several suspicious vessels that had been sighted in the vicinity of Barnegat. This promised action so strongly that a cheer went up from the crew. This time even the officers joined in.

Very shortly after came the order "All hands on the cat falls," at which every man Jack came running forward. The blue-clothed figures poured up the companion-ways like rats out of a sinking ship, for "all hands on the cat falls" means up anchor, and up anchor meant new experiences, perhaps a brush with a Spanish man-of-war or the capture of a Spanish prize. The anchor was yanked up and guided into place on its chocks in a hurry, and soon the "Yankee" was under way and headed southward. As we passed the "Columbia," the men of both ships stood at attention, feet together, hands at the side, heads up, silent. So a ship is saluted in the United States Navy, a ceremony dignified and impressive, though not as soul-stirring as the American cheer.

The "Scuttle Butt Navigators," or, as the

WE GET ORDERS TO GO SOUTH.

"Yankee" boys called them, the Rumor Committee, were very busy that bright day in May. According to them we were to sail seaward and discover Cervera's fleet, the whereabouts of which was then unknown. We were to sail south and bombard Havana. The older, wiser heads laughed at such rumors, and said it was foolishness, but all were ready and anxious to listen to the wildest tales.

All the time the ship was getting under way the routine work was going on. The sweepers had obeyed the order given by the boatswain's mate, accompanied by the pipe peculiar to that order, "Gun-deck sweepers, clean sweep fore and aft; sweepers, clean your spit kits."

At twenty minutes past nine the bugle sounded the first or officers' call to quarters, a call that sounded like "Get your sword on, get your sword on, get your sword on, get your sword on, get your sword on right away!" Ten minutes later came "assembly," and the men rushed to their places at the guns and their stations in the powder divisions.

After our division had been mustered, "Long Tommy," the boatswain's mate and captain of our gun, said to "Hay," "I think we'll have some shooting to-day. I saw the gunners' mates rigging a target."

"Good!" said "Hay," "what does it look like?"

"Why," explained Tommy, "it's a triangular sail, having a black spot painted in the middle, supported by a raft, also triangular, which is floated by three barrels, one at each corner."

"Can't be very big," said "Stump."

"About ten feet at the base, tapering to a point. The red flag that flies from the top is perhaps fourteen feet from the water, I should say."

"And they expect us to hit that?" broke in "Lucky bag Kennedy."

"Of course," said Tommy the confident, "and we shall."

As soon as the officers of the different divisions had returned from the bridge, where they had been to report, the quick, sharp bugle call which summons the crew to general quarters was sounded.

As the first notes were heard, the men scattered as if a bomb with a visible burning fuse had fallen in their midst. Some hurried to lead out the hose, some to get the gun sights and firing lanyards, some to get belts and revolvers for the guns' crews, some down into the hot, dark magazines, and some to open up the magazine hoists. All was apparent confusion, but was in reality perfect discipline. Soon boxes of shell were ready by the guns, but the order "load" had not yet been given.

The triangular target was then lowered over the side and cast loose. In a few minutes the six-pounders on the spar deck began to bark. "Getting the range, I guess," said "Hod," who had sneaked over from the powder division to get a look at the target.

"Pretty near it," replied "Stump," as a shot splashed close to the triangular piece of canvas.

"Here comes Scully," some one whispered; "now we'll have a chance."

"The captain says fire when ready, at 1,500 yards," said Scully, saluting Mr. Greene, the officer of the division. "Captain says, sir, instruct your men to shoot at the top of the roll, and a little over, rather than under the target," continued he, saluting again.

"Port battery take stations for exercise, load, set your sights at 1,500 yards, and when ready, fire." Mr. Greene's orders came sharp and clear; there was never any misunderstanding of them.

Most of us of Number Eight's gun crew had never stood near a big gun when it spoke, and most of us dreaded it and felt inclined to run away out of ear-shot. It was our business to stand by, however, so we stood by while Tommy, firing lanyard in hand, sighted the machine.

"Right!" he sung out to "Stump" and "Flagg," who were at the training wheels. "Right handsomely," added Tommy, working the elevating gear, as the gun moved slowly round. The gun roared and jumped back on its mount six or eight inches, but promptly slid back again—forced back by powerful springs. The shell sped on its way, humming as it went, and struck a little short of the target, sending up a great fountain as it was exploded by the impact with the water.

"Hay" pulled the breech lever and the breech plug came out, allowing "Stump," who wore heavy gloves for the purpose, to extract the empty shell. This he dropped in the concrete waterway, then ran to his place at the training wheel; a fresh shell had been put in the gun, meanwhile, and it was ready for business again. A number of good shots were made by different gunners. Enough to show that, amateur tars that we were, there was the making of good gunners in us. As the "Kid," in his overweening confidence, said, "Ain't we peaches? When we get down south we will have a little target practise, and the 'dagos' will be so scared that they will haul down their colors right away."

During the day we steamed slowly along, a bright lookout being kept by the men at the foremast-head for suspicious steamers. After dinner at eight bells (12 o'clock), the smoking lamp, which hangs near the scuttle butt aft, was kept lighted about fifteen minutes. Smoking is allowed aboard only when the smoking lamp is lighted, and as "Hay" was wont to say, it was lighted "when you did not want to smoke." At ten minutes past one "turn to" was piped by the boatswain's mates, followed by the call for sweepers. Then came the order, "Stand by your scrub and wash clothes." So the "Kid" and I hastened forward, both anxious to see if our initial clothes-washing venture was a success. We had depended on the sun to bleach our much be-scrubbed clothes, but—well—I would have left them where they were if I could. As for the "Kid's"—after holding them off at arm's length for a while, he remarked, "Why, I would not use such rags to clean my bicycle at home," and threw them overboard. He was always a reckless chap.

The infantry drill we had at afternoon quarters at 1:30, served to keep us busy. The same thing had been gone through on the "New

Hampshire" many a time and oft. We found it rather difficult to march straight and keep a good line on a swaying deck. So we were kept at it until we had got the hang of it. We were still parading to and fro on the spar deck, when some one sighted land off the starboard bow. The dismissal call was given none too soon, for the curiosity as to what we were heading for made discipline lax and attention far from close.

We soon learned that this was Block Island.

The gig was lowered, and the captain and mail orderly went ashore.

"Now we'll get our real orders," said Potter. "Ho! for the Spanish main," he shouted, forgetting his narrow escape of the day before.

"It will be Ho! for the ship's brig, and Ho! for five days on bread and water, if you don't look out," said "Stump," dryly.

About dark, the gig came back again, bringing the captain in it and the mail orderly—but no mail, and how we did long for a word from home. A scrap of newspaper, even, would be a blessing.

We had just sat down to evening mess when the order, "All hands on the gig falls!" was given, and the master-at-arms chased us off the gun deck. Soon the measured tread of many feet could be heard, and then the order was

"THE GIG WAS LOWERED" (page 50).

"THE MEN ON THE STAGES" (page 78).

WE GET ORDERS TO GO SOUTH.

given by the officer of the deck to the coxswain of the gig, "Secure your boat for sea."

So we were to go off again. Where?

Within a short time we were under way again. The usual watches were set, but very few of the boys went below. The mere rumor that the enemy was prowling along the coast was enough to prevent sleep. My watch went on duty at four o'clock. We were not called in the usual way, by the boatswain's whistle, but each man was roused separately. This in itself was sufficient to lend an air of intense interest to the scene.

On reaching the deck I found that the night had grown stormy. A chill wind was blowing off the coast, rendering pea coats and watch caps extremely comfortable. A fine rain began to fall shortly after four, and by the time I had taken my post forward as a lookout it had increased to a regular squall.

The "Yankee" was a splendid sea boat, but in the course of an hour the choppy waves kicked up by the storm set her to bobbing about like the proverbial cork. The gloom of the night had changed to a blackness that made it impossible to see an arm's length away. Standing on the starboard bridge, I could scarcely distinguish the faint white foam gathered under the forefoot. Aft there was nothing visible save a length of stay which seemingly began at nothing and ended in darkness.

The howling of the wind through the taut cordage of the foremast, the sullen plunging of the ship's hull in the trough of the sea, the rise to a wave crest and the poising there before falling once more, the smell of the dank salt air, and the occasional spurt of spray over the leaning bow, all made a scene so novel to me that I forgot Spanish ships and my duty and stood almost entranced.

It was a dereliction for which I was to suffer. In the midst of my reverie a hand was suddenly placed upon my shoulder and I heard a familiar voice exclaim sternly:

"Lookout, what do you mean by sleeping on post? Why did you not report that light?"

It was Captain Brownson!

Asleep on post! The accusation was grave enough to startle me, and I lost no time in stammering a denial. Luckily, the discovery of the strange light, which was just faintly visible dead ahead, occupied the commander's attention for the moment and I escaped further rebuke.

Captain Brownson hurried to the bridge and presently word was passed to go to quarters at once. The ports were opened, ammunition

WE GET ORDERS TO GO SOUTH.

made ready for both the main and secondary batteries, and the crew stood at their guns in readiness for action. It was a very impressive sight, the grim weapons just showing in the dim lantern light, the great cartridges standing close to the breeches, the men quiet and steady, their faces showing anxiety but perfect self-control.

I was proud to belong to such a crew, for the majority thought that an action was imminent, and perhaps a superior foe to be fought, yet there was no sign of that fear which is supposed to attack the novice in battle. It was a convincing proof of American bravery and self-reliance.

In the meantime the engines had been called on for full speed, and the ship throbbed and swayed with the increased power. Extra men were presently sent below to the fire room, and it soon became evident that we were in actual chase of the suspicious vessel. From my station at the after port gun I was enabled to catch an occasional glimpse of the sea through the open port.

The squall had passed in part and the night was growing lighter. The rain still fell, though fitfully, and at times a dash of water entered the port, besprinkling gun and crew and fighting tackle, leaving great drops that glistened like dew in the waning light of the lanterns. Alongside, white-capped waves raced with the ship.

As the gloom lightened, the horizon spread, and presently, away in the distance, a dark spot, like a smudge upon a gray background, became visible. "Long Tommy," attached to my gun, leaned far out of the port with an exclamation of excitement.

"By George! it's another ship," he added.

"We are in a nest of the Dagoes," cried young Potter, rather wildly. "We have run into an ambuscade."

"You've got a great chance to become a dead hero," remarked the first gun captain dryly.

Word was passed from above to break out more shell, and presently the navigator slipped down the ladder and made a close inspection of the different five-inch guns. As he went from crew to crew he gave whispered instructions to the officers in charge.

"The old man expects trouble this trip," whispered Tommy. He coolly stripped off his shirt and stood, half-naked, the muscles of his athletic chest and arms gleaming like white marble in the uncertain light. Most of us followed his example, and the spectacle of the swaying groups of men, bared for action, added a dramatic tinge to the scene.

WE GET ORDERS TO GO SOUTH.

Below, the powerful engines throbbed with a pulsation that set every bolt and joint creaking, the strident echoes of the firemen's shovels could be heard scraping against the iron floor, and little whistlings of steam came like higher notes in the general tune. Even the noises of the ship were strange and weird and impressive.

The crews had been standing in readiness at their stations for almost an hour when it suddenly became noticeable that the darkness of night was giving way before a gradual dawn. The glimmering flame in the lanterns faded and waned, objects buried in gloom began to assume shape, and the edges of the open ports grew sharp and more defined. Constant waiting brought a relaxation of discipline, and the members of the different crews grouped about the ports and eagerly searched for the chase.

The smudge on the horizon had long since disappeared, but directly ahead could be seen the faint outlines of a steamer. A dense cloud of smoke was pouring from her funnel, and it was plainly apparent that she was making every effort to escape. This in itself was enough to stamp her identity, and we shook our clenched fists exultantly after her.

The night broke rapidly. In the east a rosy tinge proclaimed the coming sun. Just as the first glitter of the fiery rim appeared above the horizon, a gray, damp mist swept across the water, coming like an impenetrable wall between the "Yankee" and the chase.

CHAPTER V.

A WILD GOOSE CHASE.

A howl of disappointment went up from the crew.

"Oh, if she was only within range," cried "Hay," smiting the breech of the five-inch rifle with his hand. "Just one shot, just one shot."

"Guns' crews will remain at stations," ordered the first lieutenant from near the ladder. "Stand by, men. Be ready for instant action."

"Hurray! the old man won't give it up," cheered "Stump," under his voice. "That's the stuff. Now, if only that measly fog lifts and we get a trifle nearer, we'll do something for the old flag."

The minutes passed slowly. It was heartbreaking work, this waiting and watching, and there was not one of the "Yankee's" crew but would have given a year's pay to have seen the mist lift long enough to bring us within range.

Suddenly, just as the fervent wish was

trembling on our lips, "Hod Marsh," who was near the port, cried out joyfully:

"She's fading, fellows, she's fading!"

Like a theatre curtain being slowly raised, the mist lifted from the surface of the water. Little by little the expanse of ocean became visible, and at last we, who were watching eagerly, saw the hull of a steamer appear, followed by masts and stack and upper rigging. An exclamation of bitter disappointment came from Tommy. "Durned if it ain't an old tramp!" he groaned. "Fellows, we are sold."

And so it proved.

The fog lifted completely in the course of an hour and we secured a good view of our "will o' the wisp" of the night's chase. It was a great lumbering tramp, as high out of the water as a barn, and as weather-stained as a homeward-bound whaler. She slouched along like a crab, each roll of the hull showing streaks of marine grass and barnacles. There was little of man-o'-war "smartness" in her make-up, of a verity.

For several days the "Yankee" cruised up and down the coast between Delaware Breakwater and Block Island. Many vessels were sighted, and on two occasions it was considered expedient to sound "general quarters," but nothing came of it. We finally concluded that the enemy were fighting shy of the vicinity of New York, and all began to long for orders to the southward.

Drill followed drill during these waiting days. Target practice was held whenever practicable, and the different guns' crews began to feel familiar with the rapid-fire rifles.

The men, accustomed to a life of ease and plenty, found this first month's work an experience of unparalleled hardship.

Their hands, better fitted for the grasp of pen and pencil, were made sore and stiff by the handling of hawsers, chains, and heavy cases. Bandages on hands, feet, and, in some cases, heads, were the popular form of adornment, and the man who did not have some part of his anatomy decorated in this way was looked upon as a "sloper," or one who ran away from work. For how could any one do his share without getting a finger jammed or a toe crushed?

The work that was done, too, during this month of cruising along the coasts of Long Island and New Jersey was hard and incessant. Drills of all kinds were frequent, and sleep at a premium.

The "Yankee" at this time was attached to the Northern Patrol Fleet, of which Commodore

Howell was the commander. It was her business to cruise along the coast from Block Island south to Delaware Breakwater, and watch for suspicious vessels. This duty made constant movement necessary, and unwearying vigilance on the part of the lookouts imperative.

Rainy, foggy weather was the rule, and "oilers" and rubber boots the prevailing fashion in overclothing. Sea watches were kept night and day; half of the crew being on duty all the time, and one watch relieving the other every four hours.

The watch " on deck " or on duty on a stormy night found it very tedious waiting for the " watch below " to come and relieve them. The man who could tell a story or sing a song was in great demand, and the man who could get up a " Yankee " song was a popular hero. The night after our wild goose chase, described in the last chapter, the port watch had the " long watch " ; that is, the watch from 8 p.m. to midnight, and from four to eight the next morning —which allowed but four hour's sleep.

It was raining and the decks were wet and slippery. The water dripped off the rims of our sou'westers in dismal fashion, and the fog hung like a blanket around the ship, while the sea lapped her sides unseen. Our fog-horn

A WILD GOOSE CHASE.

tooted at intervals, and everything was as damp, dark, and forlorn as could be.

A knot of men were gathered under the lee of the after deckhouse, huddled together for warmth and companionship. There was "Stump," "Bill," Potter, and a number of others.

"Say! can't any one sing, or tell a yarn, or whistle a tune, or dance a jig?" said "Bill" in a muffled tone. "If some one does not start some kind of excitement I will go to sleep in my tracks, and Doctor 'Gangway' says I mustn't sleep out of doors." His speech ended in a fit of coughing and a succession of sneezes.

"Here, 'Morse,' give us that new song of yours," said "Steve," as another oilskinned figure joined the group. "Morse" and "Steve" were our chief song writers. Each sat on a quarter six-pounder, one on the starboard, the other on the port. "I will, if you chaps will join in the chorus," answered "Morse." "No, thank you," he added, as some one handed him an imaginary glass. "*Nature* has wet my whistle pretty thoroughly to-night." "Stump," in his most impressive manner, stepped forward, and in true master-of-ceremonies style introduced our entertainer. He was enlarging on the undoubted merits of the composer and singer, and had waxed really eloquent, when a strong gust of wind blew the water that lodged in the awning squarely down his neck. This dampened his ardor but not our spirits.

"Morse," like the good fellow he was, got up and sang this song to the tune of " Billy Magee Magaw " :

When the "Yankee" goes sailing home again,
    Hurrah! Hurrah!
We'll forget that we're "Heroes" and just be men,
    Hurrah! Hurrah!
The girls will giggle, the boys will shout,
We'll all get a bath and be washed out,
And we'll all feel gay when
The "Yankee" goes sailing home.

The city bells will peal for joy,
    Hurrah! Hurrah!
To welcome home each wandering boy,
    Hurrah! Hurrah!
And all our sisters and cousins and girls
Will say "Ain't they darlings?" and "*See* the pearls!"
So we'll all feel gay when
The "Yankee" goes sailing home.

Our patrolling cruise will soon be o'er,
    Hurrah! Hurrah!
We'll be happy the moment our feet touch shore,
    Hurrah! Hurrah!
And "Cutlets" and "Hubbub" and all the rest
May stick to the calling they're fitted for best,
But *we'll* all feel gay when
The "Yankee" goes sailing home.

A WILD GOOSE CHASE.

Even " Bill " was able to find voice enough to shout " Good! " and give " Morse " a resounding slap on his wet oilskinned shoulder. The song voiced our sentiments exactly, and cheered us a lot. None of us believed that " Our patrolling cruise would soon be o'er," however, and hardly a man would have taken his discharge had it been offered to him that moment. We had put our names to the enlistment papers and had promised to serve Uncle Sam on his ship the " Yankee " faithfully. We had gone into this thing together, and we would see it through together. Still we would " All feel gay when the ' Yankee ' goes sailing home."

"That reminds me of a story," began Potter, when " Long Tommy," the boatswain's mate of the watch, interrupted with, " Potter, take the starboard bridge. I will send a man to relieve you at the end of an hour." So Potter went forward to relieve his mate, who had stood an hour of lookout duty on the starboard end of the bridge.

He went forward, swaying with the motion of the ship, his oilskin trousers making a queer, grating noise as one leg rubbed against the other, and " Stump " said, " I'll bet he won't stay with us long; he talks too much." A prophetic remark, as future events proved.

The group broke up after this. Some who were not actually on lookout duty went into the hot fire room, and after taking off their outer clothing, tried to snatch a few winks of sleep. The "watch on deck" was not allowed to go below at night, so the only shelter allowed us was the fire room and the main companion-way. The latter could hold but a few men, and the only alternative was the fire or "drum" room, into which the heat and gas from the furnaces ascended from the bowels of the ship, making it impossible for a man to breathe the atmosphere there for more than half an hour at a time. The after wheel-house was sometimes taken advantage of by the more venturesome of the boys, but the risk was great, for "Cutlets" was continually prowling around, and the man found taking shelter there would receive tongue lashings hard to bear, with abuse entirely out of proportion to the offence.

A little before twelve o'clock we heard the boatswain's pipe, and the long drawn shout, " On deck all the starboard watch," and " All the starboard watch to muster." So we knew that we would soon be relieved, and would be able to take the much-needed four hours' sleep in our "sleeping bags," as "Hay" called them. The starboard men came slowly up, rubbing their eyes, buttoning their oilskins, and tying their sou'westers on by a string under their chins as they walked.

"Hurry up there, will you?" calls out a port watch man, as the men of the other watch sleepily climb the ladder. "Get a move on and give us a chance to get out of this beastly wet." A sharp retort is given, and the men move on in the same leisurely way. The men of both watches are hardly in the best of humors. It is not pleasant to be waked up at midnight to stand a four hours' watch in the rain and fog, nor is it the most enjoyable thing in life to be delayed, after standing a four hours' watch in the rain, realizing all the time that each minute of waiting takes that precious time from the scant four hours' sleep.

But finally "all the watch" is piped, and we go below and flop into our hammocks, to sleep as soundly and dreamlessly as babies. A sailor will sleep like a dead man through all kinds of noises and calls, but the minute his own watch is called he is wide awake in an instant, from sheer force of habit.

So when the boatswain's mate went around with his pipe, singing out as he dodged in and out among the swinging hammocks, "On deck all the port watch," each of us jumped out of his swaying bed and began to climb into his damp clothes and stiff "oilers." We then made our way through the darkness, often bumping our heads on the bottom of hammocks, and earning sleepy but strongly worded rebukes from the occupants; colliding with stanchions, and stubbing our toes on ring bolts and hatch covers. All arrived at length, formed an unsteady line on the forecastle deck, and answered to our names as they were called by the boatswain's mate. So began another day's work on one of Uncle Sam's ships.

It was Sunday, and after a while the fog lifted and the sun came out strong and clear. All the men who were off duty came on deck to bask in the sun, and to get dried and thawed out.

"Steve" poked his uncombed, sleepy head through the "booby" hatch cover. "Well, this is something like! If the 'old man' will let us take it easy after inspection, I won't think life in the navy is so bad after all."

"Well, inspection and general muster and the reading of the ship's bible will take up most of the morning," said gunner's mate "Patt," as he emerged from the hatch after "Steve," wiping his grimy hands on a wad of waste, for he had been giving the guns a rub. "And if we don't have to go chasing an imaginary Spaniard or

A WILD GOOSE CHASE.

lug coal from the after hold forward, we'll be in luck," he continued.

"What about the 'ship's bible'? What is 'general muster'?" queried half a dozen of us.

"Why," said "Patt," "the ship's bible is the book of rules and regulations of the United States Navy. It is read once a month to the officers and crew of every ship in the navy. The officers and crew will be mustered aft—you'll see—the deck force and engineer force on the port side, the petty officers on the starboard side forward, the commissioned officers on the starboard side aft, and the marines athwartships aft. This forms three sides to a square. See?"

"I don't see the use of all this," broke in the irreverent "Kid." "Do we have to stand there and have war articles fired at us?"

"That's what, 'Kid,'" replied "Patt," good-naturedly.

"After all hands have taken their places," continued our informant, "the 'old man' will walk down the galley ladder in that dignified way of his, followed by the executive officer. 'Mother Hubbub' will then open the blue-covered book that he carries, and read you things that will make your hair stand on end and cause you to consider the best wording for your last will and testament." "Patt" was very impressive, and we stood with open mouths and staring eyes.

"When old 'Hubbub' opens the book, all hands, even the captain, will take off their hats and stand at attention. Then the war articles will be read to you. You will learn that there are twenty-seven or more offences for which you are liable to be shot—such as sleeping on post, desertion, disobedience, wilful waste of Government property, and so forth; you will be told that divine service is recommended whenever possible—in short, you are told that you must be good, and that if you are not there will be the deuce to pay. Then the captain will turn to 'Scully' and say, 'Pipe down,' whereupon 'Scully' and the other bosun's mates will blow a trill on their pipes, and all hands will go about their business."

So concluded our oracle.

"Gee whiz!" said the "Kid." "I nearly got into trouble the other night, for I almost dozed when I was on the buoy. I'm not used to getting along on eleven hours' sleep in forty-eight yet," he added, apologetically.

We all looked forward to "general muster" with a good deal of interest, and when it occurred, and the captain had inspected our persons, clothes, the ship, and mess gear, we decided

A WILD GOOSE CHASE.

that "Patt's" description fitted exactly, and were duly impressed with its solemnity.

We found to our sorrow that we of Number Eight's crew were not to enjoy sunshine undisturbed, but were soon put to work carrying coal in baskets from the after hold forward, and dumping it in the bunker chutes.

This work had been going on almost every day, and all day, since we left Tompkinsville. The coal was in the after hold and was needed in the bunkers forward, so every piece had to be shovelled into bushel baskets, hoisted to the gun deck, and carried by hand to the chute leading to the port and starboard bunkers. A dirty job it was, that not only blackened the men, but covered the deck, the mess gear, the paint work, and even the food, with coal dust.

Number Eight's crew had been at this pleasant occupation for about an hour, with the cheerful prospect of another hour of the same diversion. "Hay" was running the steam winch, "Stump" was pulling the baskets over the hatch coaming as they were hauled up by the winch, and the other five were carrying.

"Say, this is deadly slow, tiresome work," said "Flagg," who was carrying with me. "I'd give almost anything for a little excitement."

The last word had scarcely been uttered when

there came the sounds of commotion on deck. A voice cried out in sharp command, the rudder chains creaked loudly, the ship heeled over to starboard, and then we who were at the open port saw a long, snaky object shoot out from the edge of the haze and bear down upon us.

"My heaven!" shouted "Stump," "it's a torpedo boat!"

The commotion on deck had given us some warning, but the sudden dash of the long, snaky torpedo boat from out the haze came as a decided shock. For one brief moment we of the after port stood as if turned to stone, then every man ran to his quarters and stood ready to do his duty. With a cry, our second captain sprang to the firing lanyard. Before he could grasp it, however, the officer of the division was at his side.

"Stop!" he exclaimed authoritatively.

The interruption was fortunate, for, just then, a swerve of the oncoming torpedo boat revealed a small flag flying from the taffrail staff. It was the American ensign.

The reaction was great. Forgetting discipline, we crowded about the port and laughed and cheered like a lot of schoolboys. Potter, in his joy and evident relief, sent his canvas cap sailing through the air. A rebuke, not very stern, however, came from the lieutenant in charge of the division, and we shuffled back to our stations.

"Cricky! what a sell," exclaimed the second rifleman, grinning. "I was sure we had a big job on our hands this time. I'm rather glad it is one of our fellows after all."

"I'm not," spoke up young Potter, blusteringly. "What did we come out here for, hey? I say it's a confounded shame. We might have had a chance to send one of the Spaniards to the bottom."

"It may be a Dago after all," suggested "Bill," glancing from the port. "The flag doesn't mean anything. They might be flying Old Glory as a *ruse de guerre*. By George! That craft looks just like the 'Pluton.'"

We, who were watching, saw Potter's face lengthen. He peered nervously at the rapidly approaching torpedo boat, and then tried to laugh unconcernedly.

"You can't 'string' me," he retorted. "That's one of your Uncle Samuel's boats all right. See! they are going to hail us."

A bell clanged in the engine room, then the throbbing of the machinery slackened to a slow pulsation. The rudder chains rattled in their fair-leaders, and presently we were steaming along, with the torpedo craft a score of yards off our midships.

On the forward deck of the latter stood two officers clad in the uniform of the commissioned service. One placed a speaking trumpet to his lips and called out:

"Cruiser ahoy! Is that the 'Yankee'?"

"You have made a good guess," shouted Captain Brownson. "What boat is that?"

"'Talbot' from Newport. Any news? Sighted you and thought we would speak you."

Our commander assured them that we were in search of news ourselves. The "Talbot's" officers saluted and then waved a farewell.

The narrow, low-lying craft spun about in almost her own length, a series of quick puffs of dense black smoke came from the funnels, and then the haze swallowed up the whole fabric.

We were left to take our discomfiture with what philosophy we could muster. When "secure" was sounded we left our guns with a sense of great danger averted and a feeling of relief.

CHAPTER VI.

WE BECOME COAL HEAVERS.

The little strip of North American coast between Delaware Breakwater and Block Island is very interesting, and, in places, beautiful. The long beaches and bare sand dunes have a solemn beauty all their own.

Though the boys on the "Yankee" took in and appreciated the loveliness of this bit of coast, they were getting rather familiar with it and somewhat bored. They longed for "pastures new."

Summer had almost begun, but still the fog and rain held sway. The ship crept through the night like a big gray ghost—dark, swift, and, except in the densest fogs, silent. Pea-coats were an absolute necessity, and woolen gloves would have been a great comfort. All this in the blooming, beautiful month of May!

One bleak morning the starboard watch was on duty. We of the port watch had turned in at four (or, according to ship's time, eight bells).

We were glad to be between decks, and got under way for the land of Nod without delay. It seemed as if we had been asleep but a few minutes, when "Scully," chief boatswain's mate, came down the gun deck gangway, shouting loud enough to be heard a mile away: " All hands, up all hammocks; " then, as the disposition to get up was not very evident, " Show a leg there; ham and eggs for breakfast." This last was a little pleasantry that never materialized into the much-coveted and long abstained from delicacy.

The hammocks were lashed up and stowed away in the "nettings," as the lattice-like receptacles are called, leaving the deck clear for the work of the day.

Mess gear for the "watch below" had just been piped, and we were glad; even the thought of burnt oatmeal and coffee without milk was pleasant to us.

The ports were closed and the gun deck was dark and dismal. The fog oozed in through every crack and cranny, and all was very unpleasant.

Of a sudden there was a sharp reverberation that sounded so much like the report of a big gun that all hands jumped.

The course of the ship was changed, and the jingle bell sounded. The "Yankee" forged on at full speed in the direction from which the sound had come.

We all stood in expectant attitudes, listening for another report. We had about made up our minds that our ears had deceived us, when another explosion, louder and nearer than the first, reached us.

On we rushed—toward what we knew not—through a fog so thick that the water could be seen but dimly from the spar deck.

The suspense was hard to bear, and the desire to do something almost irresistible. The men unconsciously took their regular stations for action, the guns' crews gathered round their guns, the powder divisions in the neighborhood of the ammunition hoists.

" I wish Potter was here," said " Stump." " I rather think he would be white around the gills. This sort of business would give him a bad case of ' cold feet.' "

" Oh, he had ' cold feet ' a few days after we left New York, and wrote to his friends to get his discharge," said " Bill." " Got it and quit two weeks after we left New York, the duffer," added " Hay."

The " Yankee " still steamed on into the bank of fog.

" Cupid," the ship's bugler, began to play the

call for general quarters, but was stopped by a sharp command from the bridge.

What was it all about? Was it to be tragedy or farce?

Then Scully came down the starboard gangway, a broad smile on his ruddy face.

A clamoring group gathered round him instantly. "What is it?" "Is the 'old man' playing a joke on us?" "Do you suppose Cervera has got over to this side?" "Scully," overwhelmed with questions, put up his hands protestingly.

"No, no; none of those things," said he. "What do you suppose we have been doing for the last twenty minutes?"

We confessed we did not know.

"Chasing thunder claps—nothing more nor less than thunder claps! And we'll see nothing worse on this coast," he added sententiously, as soon as he could get his breath.

The wind rose, and while it blew away the fog in part, it kicked up a nasty sea, in which the "Yankee" wallowed for hours, waiting for the fog to clear enough to make the channel and enter New York harbor. It seemed we had been heading for New York, and we did not know it. It was not the custom aboard that hooker to give the men any information.

"THE 'YANKEE' DROPPED HER ANCHOR OFF TOMPKINSVILLE" (page 77).

WE BECOME COAL HEAVERS.

When we learned for sure that we were bound for New York, our joy was beyond measure.

Shore leave was the chief topic of conversation. And every man not on duty went down into his black bag, fished out his clean blues, and set to work sewing on watch marks and cap ribbons. For Jack must be neat and clean when he goes ashore.

The mud-hook was dropped in the bay off Tompkinsville, Thursday, May 26th, seventeen days after we left the navy yard. It seemed seventeen months.

An "anchor watch" of sixteen men was set for the night, and most of us turned in early to enjoy the first good sleep for many weary days.

All hands were turned out at five o'clock. We woke to find a big coal barge on either side of the ship.

After breakfast the order "turn to" was given. "All hands coal ship, starboard watch on the starboard lighter, port watch on the port lighter." From seven o'clock in the morning till twelve o'clock that night, the crew of the "Yankee"—aforetime lawyers, physicians, literary men, brokers, merchants, students, and clerks—men who had never done any harder work than play football, or row in a shell—coaled ship without any rest, other than the three half hours at meal times. About the hardest, dirtiest work a man could do.

The navy style of coaling is different from that customary in the merchant service. In the latter, the dirty work is done in the quickest, easiest way possible. The ship is taken to a coal wharf and the coal is slid down in chutes, or barges are run alongside and great buckets, hoisted by steam, swing the black lumps into the hold or bunker.

The navy style, as practised on the "Yankee," was quite different. The barges were brought alongside, the men divided into gangs—some to go in the hold of the barge, some to go on the platforms, some to carry on the ship herself. The barge gang shovelled the coal into bushel baskets; these were carried to the men on the stages; and the latter passed them from one to the other, to the gun deck; finally, the gang on the vessel carried the baskets to the bunker holes, and dumped them. The ship was well provided with hoisting machines, but, for some reason, this help was not permitted us.

It was a long, inexpressibly dreary day's work, and though undertaken cheerfully and with less complaining than would have been believed possible, the drudgery of it was a thing not easily forgotten. Before the day had ended, all hope of getting ashore was lost, for we were told that no liberty would be given.

The following day and half of our stay in New York harbor was spent in the same way—shovelling, lifting, and carrying coal. The eyes of many of us were gladdened by the sight of friends and relatives, who were allowed aboard when mess gear was piped, and put off when "turn to" sounded. We were pleased to see our friends, but our friends, on the contrary, seemed shocked to see us. One dainty girl came aboard, and, as she came up the gangway, asked for a forecastle man. The word was passed for him. He had just finished his stint of coaling, and was as black as a negro. In his haste to see his sister, he neglected to clean up, and appeared before her in his coal heaver's make-up.

"You, Will? I won't believe it! I won't, I won't, I won't!" And for a second she covered her face with her hands. Then she picked out the cleanest spot on his grimy countenance and kissed him there, while we looked on in envy.

The "Yankee" at last receiving orders to sail for the front, left Tompkinsville May 29th. We passed out of the Narrows with a feeling of relief. The work we had just finished was the hardest we had ever experienced. It was particularly tantalizing because we were almost in sight of our homes, but could not visit them. A starving man suffers more from hunger if pleasant food is placed within sight, but beyond his reach.

However, we were to go to the front at last, and we rejoiced at the prospect of being really useful to our country.

The following day, Decoration Day, dawned pleasantly, both wind and weather being all that could be desired.

Directly after dinner we were sent to quarters for target practice. The target was dropped astern, and the ship steamed ahead to the required distance. Word was given to the marines manning the six-pounders to prove their skill.

The port forecastle six-pounder, using a shell containing cordite, a powerful English explosive, was in charge of a marine corporal named J. J. Murray, who acted as captain of the gun. After firing several rounds with marked success, Murray saw that the gun was loaded for another trial.

Standing at the breech, he steadied the gun with his left arm and shoulder, seized the pistol-grip, placed his finger on the trigger, and then slowly and carefully brought the target within the sighting line in readiness to fire.

WE BECOME COAL HEAVERS.

The other members of the gun's crew were at their proper stations. Numbers 2 and 3, respectively second captain and first loader and shellman, were directly behind the corporal. They saw him steady the piece again, take another careful aim, then noted that his finger gave a quick tug at the trigger.

The result was a dull click but no explosion.

The corporal stepped back from his place in vexation. He had succeeded in getting a fine "bead" just as the cartridge failed.

"Blast the English ammunition!" he exclaimed. "It's no good."

The other men at the gun nodded approval. Their experience bore out the corporal's assertion. They also knew that the cordite cartridges were not adapted to American guns, and should not have been used. But they were marines and they were accustomed to obey orders without comment.

Captain Brownson had noticed the incident and he sent word to delay opening the breech-block until all danger of explosion had passed. After waiting some time, Corporal Murray proceeded to extract the shell. He took his place at the breech, while No. 2 unlocked the plug and swung it open.

"Now we'll see what is the matter," he began. "I guess it is another case of——"

He never finished the sentence. With a frightful roar the defective cartridge exploded, sending fragments of shell and parts of the breech-block into the corporal's face and chest. He was hurled with terrific force to the deck, where he lay motionless, mortally wounded.

Numbers 2 and 3 of the unfortunate gun's crew did not escape, the former being struck down with the hand lever, which penetrated his arm. The injured men received prompt attention from the surgeon and his assistants, but Corporal Murray was beyond mortal aid. He died ten minutes after the accident.

He was a good soldier, jolly and light-hearted, and a great favorite with the crew. The peculiar feeling of antagonism which is supposed to exist between the sailors and marines did not obtain in his case.

In the navy the hammock which serves the living as a bed by night is also their coffin and their shroud. It so served Corporal Murray.

Shortly after four bells (six o'clock) on the evening of the day on which the accident occurred, the boatswain's mate sent the shrill piping of his whistle echoing through the ship,

"WITH A FRIGHTFUL ROAR THE DEFECTIVE CARTRIDGE EXPLODED" (*page* 82).

following it with the words, doleful and long drawn out:

"All hands shift-ft-ft into clean-n-n blue and stand by to bury the dead-d-d!"

When the crew assembled on the gun deck in obedience to the call, the sun was just disappearing beyond the edge of the distant horizon. Its last rays entered the open port, showing to us the dead man's figure outlined under an American flag. The body had been placed upon a grating in front of an open port, and several men were stationed close by in readiness to launch it into the sea.

The ceaseless swaying of the ship in the trough of the sea, the engines having been stopped, set the lines of blue uniformed men swinging and nodding, and, as the surgeon, Dr. McGowan, read the Episcopal service, it seemed in the half light as if every man were keeping time with the cadence.

The words of the service, beautiful and impressive under such novel circumstances, echoed and whispered along the deck, and at the sentence, "We commit this body to the deep," the grating was raised gently and, with a peculiar *swish*, the body, heavily weighted, slid down to the water's edge and plunged sullenly into the sea. A moment more and the service was finished, the bugler sounding "pipe down." A salute, three times repeated, was fired by sixteen men of the marine guard.

. . . .

The voyage down the coast was utilized in making good men-o'-war's men of the "Yankee's" crew. Captain Brownson believes thoroughly in the efficacy of drill, and he lost no time in living up to his belief. When all the circumstances are taken into consideration, the task allotted to the captain of the "Yankee" by the fortunes of war, was both peculiar and difficult.

On his return from Europe, where he had been sent to select vessels for the improvised navy, he was ordered by the Navy Department at Washington to take command of the auxiliary cruiser "Yankee." This meant that he was to assume charge of a ship hastily converted from an ordinary merchant steamer, and to fight the battles of his country with a crew composed of youths and men whose whole life and training had hitherto followed totally different lines.

It was a "licking of raw material into shape" with a vengeance.

When the "Chesapeake" sailed forth to fight her disastrous battle with the British ship "Shannon," her crew was made up of men un-

WE BECOME COAL HEAVERS.

trained in the art of war. The result was the most humiliating naval defeat in the history of the United States. The same fate threatened Captain Brownson. There was this difference in the cases, however. The " Chesapeake " had little time for drilling, while the " Yankee " was fully six weeks in commission before her first shot was fired in action. Every minute of those six weeks was utilized.

During the trip down the coast from New York general quarters were held each day, and target practice whenever the weather permitted. In addition to these drills the crew was exercised in man and arm boats, abandon ship, fire drill, infantry drill, and the many exercises provided by the naval regulations. Before the "Yankee" had been in the Gulf Stream two days, the various guns' crews were almost letter-perfect at battery work. As it happened, the value of good drilling was soon to be demonstrated.

As we neared Cuba, the theatre of our hopes and expectations, we were scarcely able to control ourselves. The bare possibility of seeing real war within a few days made every man the victim of a consuming impatience. Rumors of every description were rife, and the many weird and impossible tales invented by the ship's cook and the captain's steward—the men-o'-war oracles—would have put even Baron Munchausen to the blush.

The Rumor Committee, otherwise known as the "Scuttle-butt Navigators," to which every man on board was elected a life member the moment he promulgated a rumor, was soon actively engaged, and it was definitely settled that the "Yankee" was to become the flagship of the whole fleet, our captain made Lord High Admiral, and the whole Spanish nation swept off the face of the globe, in about thirteen and a half seconds by the chronometer.

CHAPTER VII.

WE ENTER THE "THEATRE OF WAR."

The shrill pipe of the bosun's whistle, followed by the order "All hands to muster," reached our ears a day or two out from New York. We were enjoying an hour of well-earned leisure, so it was with reluctance that we obeyed and went aft on the gun deck. All hands are seldom called to muster, so we knew that something of importance was in the wind.

After the three-sided hollow square had been formed, the captain appeared. The small men stood on tip-toe, and the tall men craned their necks.

"We are about to enter the theatre of war," said the captain, in his sharp, decisive way, "and I expect every man to do his duty, to redouble his efforts to preserve discipline, to perfect drills. Drills will, of a necessity, be frequent and hard. I would have you understand that our best protection is the fire from our own guns. The more rapid and accurate our fire, the safer we shall be. Pipe down."

After we had been dismissed, the men formed little groups and discussed the captain's speech.

"I like the 'old man's' talk," said the "Kid," condescendingly; "it's to the point and short. But how in the name of common sense are we going to find time to drill with more frequency? Three times a day and once or more at night, allows us just about time enough to eat and do the necessary routine work, to say nothing about sleeping. Clear ship, general quarters, and fire drill during the day, and general quarters after ten last night. That's already somewhat frequent, methinks," he concluded, suppressing a yawn.

"Well, if we are to have any scraps," said "Bill," "we certainly must know how to work the ship and the guns. For, as the skipper said, 'our own fire is our best protection.'"

We bowled along at a good fifteen-knot gait, day after day and night after night. The weather was magnificent and the climate delightful. It was full moon, and such a moon as few of us had seen before—so bright that letters could be and were written by her silvery light.

Though drills of all sorts were of constant occurrence, there were times after mess when we

WE ENTER THE "THEATRE OF WAR."

could "caulk off" and enjoy the glorious weather. Our experience of bad weather along the coast of New Jersey and Long Island had given us keen zest for the good conditions we were now enjoying. We were sailing along in the warm waters of the Gulf Stream—the Gulf weed peculiar to that current slipping by as we forged through it. "Stump," "Dye," of Number Eight's gun crew, a witty chap and a good singer, "Hay," and I were leaning over the taffrail, looking into the swirling water made by the propeller's thrust, when "Dye" remarked: "This is the queerest water I ever saw in all my days; it looks like the bluing water our laundress used to make, with the suds mixed in."

The smooth sea was dark and clear as could be, but where churned by the propeller it turned to the color of turquoise.

"I really believe," said "Bill," as he joined the group, "that we could use it to turn our whites blue."

It was a delight and marvel to us all; we would have liked nothing better than to have spent hours gazing at these wonderful colors.

As we stood absorbed in the sight before us, we were interrupted by the short, sharp ringing of the ship's bell—a dozen or more strokes given in quick succession followed, after a short pause, by two more strokes.

Some one shouted "Fire, boys!" and all hands rushed for their stations—some to the hose-reel, some below to the gun deck to close the ports, and some to the berth deck to receive the hose when it came down. We did not know whether it was drill or actual fire, but the skipper's talk of the night before gave us unusual energy, and the preparations were made in record time. The canvas hose was pulled along the deck with a swish, the nozzle grasped by the waiting hands below and carried with a run away aft on the berth deck. The fire was supposed to be raging at this point, as was indicated by the two last strokes of the alarm signal.

While the hose was being led out, sturdy arms tugged at the port lanyards and pulled them to. Others battened down the hatches, to keep the draught from adding fury to the flames.

All this was done in less time than it takes to tell it, and the men stood at their posts, perspiring and panting from the quick work.

We had hardly time to catch our breath when the order "Abandon ship" was heard. Immediately there was a scurry of feet, and a rush for the upper deck; but some stayed below to carry

These circles indicate the red and white lights of the "Ardois" system of night-signalling. They are four in number, hung one below the other on the foremast. They are lighted by electricity, and any or all may be turned on at will.

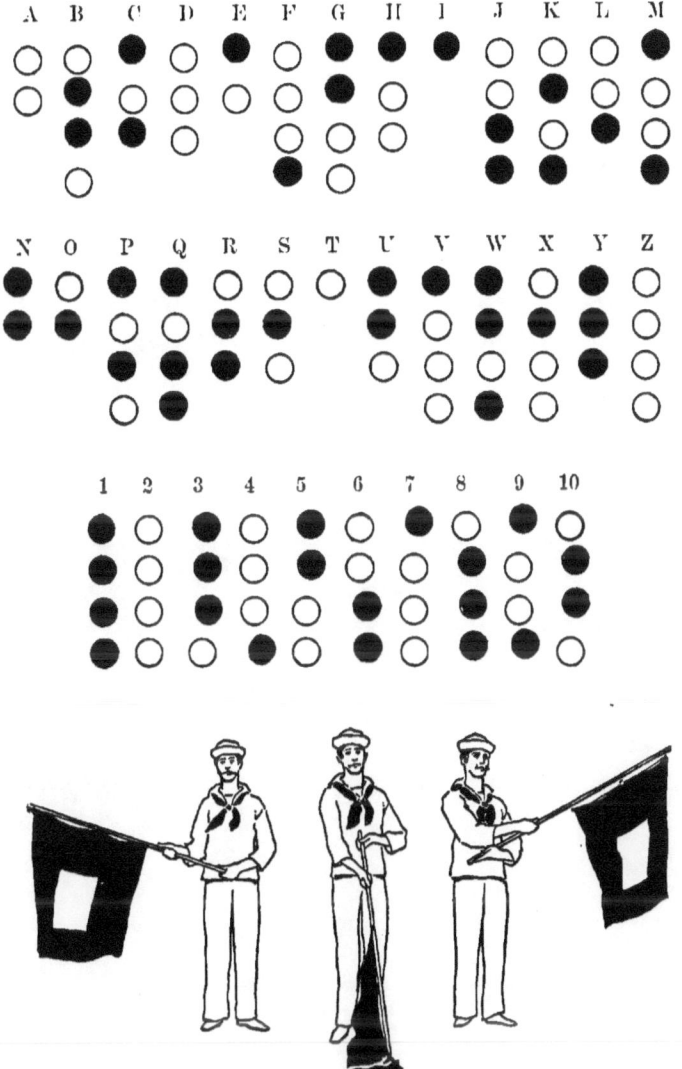

WIGWAGGING.

The whole wigwag system of signalling is made up of these three motions: to the right, one; to the left, two; in front, three. The code will be found in the Appendix.

WE ENTER THE "THEATRE OF WAR."

ship's bread and canned meats to the boats—two cases of bread and two cases of meat for the large boats, and one case of each for the smaller. The crews and passengers of each boat gathered near it. Every man had been assigned to a boat either as crew or passenger, and when the order "abandon ship" was given, every one knew instantly where to go for refuge.

Though we had already gone through this "fire drill" and "abandon ship" (one always followed the other), it had then been done in peaceful waters and in a perfunctory way. Now that we were entering "the theatre of war," we felt the seriousness of it all, and realized that what was now a mere drill might become a stern reality.

The order "Secure" was given; the hose was reeled up, the ports opened, and the provisions returned to their places in hold and store room. The men went to their quarters, and so stood till the bugler blew "retreat."

The time not devoted to drills was taken up in getting the ship ready for the serious work she was to undertake.

All woodwork on the gun deck not in actual use was carried below or thrown overboard, and the great cargo booms were either taken down and stowed safely away, where the splinters would not be dangerous, or were covered with canvas.

These preparations had a sinister look that made us realize, if we had not done so before, that this was real war that we were about to engage in—no sham battle or manœuvres.

The men went about their work more quietly and thoughtfully, for one and all now understood their responsibilities. If the ship made a record for herself, the crew would get a large share of the credit; and if she failed to do the work cut out for her, on the crew would be laid the blame. If the men behind the guns and the men running the engines did not do their work rapidly and well, disaster and disgrace would follow.

As we neared the scene of conflict, the discipline grew more and more strict. Before a man realized that he had done anything wrong, his name would be called by the master-at-arms and he would be hauled "up to the mast" for trial.

"You ought to see the gang up at the mast," said "Stump," one bright afternoon. "'Mac' and 'Hod Marsh' have gathered enough extra duty men to do all the dirty work for a month."

"What were you doing up there?" asked a bystander.

WE ENTER THE "THEATRE OF WAR."

"Why, I thought I heard my name called, and as discretion is the better part of valor, I lined up with the rest, and I was glad I did, too, for it was good sport."

"Maybe you thought it was sport, but how about the chaps that were 'pinched'? Who was up before the skipper, anyhow?"

"Oh, there was a big gang up there—I can't remember them all; 'Lucky Bag Kennedy' was there, for being late at general quarters the other day. When the captain looked at him in that fierce way of his and asked what he had to say for himself, 'Lucky Bag' said he didn't realize the time. The skipper could hardly keep his face straight. 'Four hours,' he said, and that was all there was to it."

"Poor 'Lucky Bag,'" came from all sides as "Stump" paused to take breath.

"Then there was 'Big Bill,' the water tender," continued "Stump." "He was hauled up for appearing on the spar deck without a uniform. When the skipper asked him what he had to say for himself, 'Big Bill' cleared his throat with a *woof*—you know how it sounds: the ship shakes and trembles when he does it—and the 'old man' fairly tottered under the blast. 'Big Bill' explained that he could not get a uniform big enough for him, because the paymaster could not fit him out. The captain almost grinned when he heard the excuse, and 'Big Bill'—well, he enjoyed the situation, I'll bet a month's pay."

There was a little pause here, and we heard a great voice rumbling from below. Then we knew that "Big Bill" was telling his intimates all about it, embellishing the story as only he could do.

We laughed sympathetically as the shouts of glee rose to our ears. We had all enjoyed his good-humored Irish wit.

"Well, who else was in trouble this afternoon, 'Stump'?" said "Mourner," the inquisitive.

"Oh, a lot of unfortunate duffers. Several who were put on the report for being slow in lashing up their hammocks got a couple of hours extra duty each. One or two were there because they had clothes in the 'lucky bag'—they had left them round the decks somewhere, and the master-at-arms had grabbed them. The owners had to go on the report to get the clothes out. It cost them a couple of hours each."

"Well, how did you get out of it?" said I, when "Stump" paused to breathe.

"I was nearly scared to death," he continued, after a minute or two. "My name was not

WE ENTER THE "THEATRE OF WAR."

called, and the rank thinned out till there were only a few of us left. I began to think that some special punishment was being reserved for me, and that the captain was waiting so he could think it over. What my offence was I could not imagine; my conscience was clear, I vow. As I stood there in the sun I thought over the last few days, and made a confession to myself, but couldn't think of anything very wicked. Had I unintentionally blocked a marine sentry's way and thus interfered with him in the performance of his duty? I had visions at this point of myself in the 'brig,' existing on bread and water. Had I inadvertently gone into 'Cutlet's' pet after wheel-house? I was in a brown study, conjuring up imaginary misdeeds, when a voice sounded in my ear: 'Here, my man; what do you want?' I looked around, dazed, at the captain, who stood by, the closed report book in his hand. Then I realized that my being there was a mistake, so I saluted and said, 'Nothing, sir.' "

"That's a very nice tale," said "Dye." "We'll have to get 'Mac' to verify it."

"It's straight," protested "Stump." "Ask the skipper himself if you want to."

The old boat ploughed her way through the blue waters of the Gulf Stream at the rate of from fourteen to fifteen knots an hour. The skies were clear and the sun warm and bright— a cool breeze tempered its heat and made life bearable. The ship rolled lazily in the long swell and the turquoise wake boiled astern. We steamed for days without sighting a sail or a light; we were "alone on a wide, wide sea." At times schools of dolphins would race and shoot up out of the water alongside, much to our glee. All the beauties of these tropical waters were new to us. Every school of flying fish and flock of Mother Carey's chickens brought crowds to the rail. The sunsets were glorious, though all too short, and the sunrises, if less appreciated, just as fine.

At night the guns' crews of the "watch on deck" slept round their loaded guns, one man of each crew always standing guard. The men of the powder divisions manned the lookout posts.

All hands were in good spirits, calmed somewhat, however, by the thought that soon we might be in the thick of battle, the outcome of which no man could tell.

It was during this voyage that friendships, begun on the Block Island-Barnegat cruise, were cemented. The life aboard ship tended to "show up" a man as he really was. His good and bad qualities appeared so that all might see. Was

WE ENTER THE "THEATRE OF WAR."

he good-natured, even-tempered, thoughtful, his mates knew it at once and liked him. Was he quick-tempered, selfish, uncompanionable, it was quite as evident, and he had few friends. Sterling and unsuspected qualities were brought out in many of the men.

Every man felt that we must and would stand together, and with a will do our work, be it peaceful or warlike.

Where were we bound? Were we to join the Havana blockading fleet? Were we destined for despatch and scout duty? Or were we to take part in actual conflict?

It was while we were settling these questions to our own satisfaction on the morning of June 2d, that a hail came from the lookout at the masthead forward.

"Land O!" he shouted, waving his cap. "Hurray! it's Cuba!"

The navigator, whose rightful surname had been converted by the facetious Naval Reserves into "Cutlets," for reasons of their own, lost no time in rebuking the too enthusiastic lookout.

"Aloft, there, you measly lubber! What in thunder do you mean? Have you sighted land?"

"Ye-es, sir-r," quavered the lookout.

"Then why don't you say so without adding

any conjectures of your own?" commented the irascible Lieutenant "Cutlets," severely.

The rest of the crew were too deeply interested in the vague streak of color on the horizon to pay any attention to the "wigging" of the man at the masthead. We knew that the dun-hued streak rising from the blue shadows of the ocean was Cuba, and we could think or talk of nothing else.

Somewhere beyond that towering mountain was Santiago, the port in which the flea-like squadron of Admiral Cervera was bottled up, and there was a deadly fear in our hearts that the wily Spaniard would sally forth to battle before we could join our fleet.

We pictured to ourselves the gray mountain massed high about the narrow entrance of Santiago Bay, the picturesque Morro Castle, squatting like a grim giant above the strait, and outside, tossing and bobbing upon the swell of a restless sea, the mighty semicircle of drab ships waiting, yearning for the outcoming of the Dons. We of the "Yankee," I repeat, were in an agony of dread that we would arrive too late.

Cape Maysi, the scene of many an adventurous filibustering expedition, was passed at high noon, and at eight bells in the evening the anchor was dropped off Mole St. Nicholas, a convenient port in the island of Hayti. As we steamed into the harbor we passed close to the auxiliary cruiser " St. Louis."

The anchor was scarcely on the bottom when the gig was called away. We awaited the return of Captain Brownson with impatience. The news he brought was reassuring, however. Nothing of moment had occurred since our departure from New York. Within an hour we were again out at sea, this time en route to Santiago.

There was little sleep on board that night, and when morning dawned, every man who could escape from below was on deck watching, waiting for the first glimpse of Admiral Sampson's fleet. Shortly after daylight, the squadron was sighted. The scene was picturesque in the extreme.

The gray of early dawn was just giving way before the first rays of a tropical sun. Almost hidden in the mist hovering about the coast were a number of vague spots seemingly arranged in a semicircle, the base of which was the green-covered tableland fronting Santiago. The spots were tossing idly upon a restless sea, and, as the sun rose higher, each gradually assumed the shape of a marine engine of war. Beyond them was a stretch of sandy, surf-beaten coast, and directly fronting the centre ship could be seen a narrow cleft in the hill—the gateway leading to the ancient city of Santiago de Cuba.

As we steamed in closer to the fleet we saw indications that something of importance had occurred or was about to occur. Steam launches and torpedo boats were dashing about between the ships, strings of parti-colored bunting flaunted from the signal halliards of the flagship "New York," and nearer shore could be seen one of the smaller cruisers evidently making a reconnaissance.

"We are just in time, Russ," exclaimed "Stump," jubilantly. "The fleet is getting ready for a scrap. And we'll be right in it."

I edged toward the bridge. The first news would come from that quarter. Several minutes later, Captain Brownson, who had been watching the signals with a powerful glass, closed the instrument with a snap, and cried out to the executive officer:

"Hubbard, you will never believe it."

"What's happened?"

The reply was given so low that I could catch only a few words, but it was enough to send me scurrying aft at the top of my speed. The news was startling indeed.

"STAND BY, MEN. BE READY FOR INSTANT ACTION"
(*page* 57).

CHAPTER VIII.

WE JOIN SAMPSON'S FLEET.

As the "Yankee" steamed in toward the blockading fleet off the entrance to Santiago harbor, the scurrying torpedo boats and the many little launches darting here and there like so many beetles on a pond, became more apparent, and it was plainly evident to all that something of great importance had recently happened.

The scattered remarks made by Captain Brownson on the bridge formed, when pieced together, such a wonderful bit of news that I could scarcely contain myself as I hurried aft. I wanted to stop and fling my cap into the air. I felt like dancing a jig and hurrahing and offering praise for the fact that I was an American.

As it happened, I was not the only member of the "Yankee's" crew that had overheard the "old man's" words. The second captain of the after port five-inch gun, a jolly good fellow, known familiarly as "Hay" by the boys, chanced to be under the bridge. As I raced aft on the port side he started in the same direction on the starboard side of the spar deck. His legs fairly twinkled, and he beat me to the gangway by a neck.

"What do you think?" I heard him gasp as I came up. "Talk of your heroes! Whoop! Say, I'm glad I am a son of that old flag aft there. It's the greatest thing that ever happened."

"What?" chorused a dozen voices.

"Last night——"

"Yes."

"Last night a volunteer crew——"

"Hurry up, will you?"

"Last night, or rather early this morning, a volunteer crew, under the command of a naval constructor named Hobson, took the collier 'Merrimac' into the mouth of the harbor and——"

"That old tub?" interrupted a marine who had served in the regular navy, incredulously. "Why, she's nothing but a hulk. She hasn't a gun or——"

"She didn't go in to fight," said "Hay."
"They were to block up the channel with her."

"To block up the channel?"

WE JOIN SAMPSON'S FLEET.

"Yes. Cervera and his fleet are in the harbor, you know, and the scheme was to keep them from coming out."

"Did they succeed?" chorused the whole group of eager listeners.

"Yes, but——"

The conclusion of "Hay's" sentence was drowned in a wild whoop of joy, a whoop that brought a number of other "Yankees" to the spot, and also a gesture of remonstrance from the executive officer on the bridge.

"Wait, boys," I said, gently; "you haven't heard all."

There was quiet at once.

"Hobson and his brave men succeeded in accomplishing their object, but they have paid the penalty for it."

"Not dead?" asked one in almost a whisper.

"So the captain read the signals. The 'Merrimac' went in about three o'clock this morning. It seems she reached the channel all right, but she was discovered and sent to the bottom with all on board."

"Hay" took off his cap reverently, and the others instantly followed his example. Nothing more was said. The glory of the deed was overshadowed by the supposed fate of the gallant volunteer crew.

The "Yankee" steamed in to a position designated by the flagship, and the captain went aboard to pay his respects to Admiral Sampson. A Spanish tug, flying a flag of truce, which had emerged from the harbor at noon, met one of our tugs, also flying a flag of truce, and almost immediately a string of signals went up to the signal yard of the "New York."

Then came such a burst of cheers and whistling and tossing of hats from every ship in the fleet that it seemed as if every officer and sailor in Sampson's squadron had suddenly gone daft. Like wildfire, the glorious news spread——

Hobson and his men were safe!

The tug from the harbor had brought an officer sent by Admiral Cervera himself with a message stating that the brave naval constructor and all his crew had been captured alive and were now prisoners in Morro Castle. Later, a press boat came alongside and confirmed the news through a megaphone.

The excitement on board the "Yankee," like that throughout the fleet, was tremendous. Those in the North who had received both the news of the feat and the rescue at the same time, can hardly understand the revulsion of feeling which swept through the American ships gathered off Santiago. It was like hearing from a supposed dead friend.

These heroes were comrades—nay, brothers. They wore the blue and they were fighting for Old Glory. Their praise was ours and their deed redounded to the eternal credit and fame of the American navy. Small wonder that we welcomed the news of their safety, and cheered until our throats were husky and our eyes wet with something more than mere exertion.

All hail to Richmond Pearson Hobson and his men!

Heroes all!

. . . .

During the afternoon of our arrival, when we finally secured time to look about us, we were struck with the appearance of the really formidable fleet of warships collected under Admiral Sampson's flag. For size of individual ships and weight of armor and armament, there had never been anything in the history of the United States to equal it.

The fleet consisted of the powerful battleships "Iowa," "Indiana," "Massachusetts," and "Texas," the two splendid armored cruisers "New York" and "Brooklyn," cruisers "New Orleans" and "Marblehead," converted yachts "Mayflower," "Josephine," and "Vixen," torpedo boat "Porter," cable boat "Adria," gunboat "Dolphin," and the auxiliary cruisers "St. Louis" and "Yankee."

The vessels formed a semicircular line, completely enclosing the entrance to Santiago harbor. From where the "Yankee" rested, on the right wing, a fine view of the coast could be obtained. Two insurgent camps were plainly visible—one on the beach and another in the hills, which at that point rose to the height of fully four thousand feet. Morro Castle, a grim, sullen, gray embattled fort, directly overlooking the channel, was in plain sight, and here and there could be seen little green or sand-colored mounds, marking the site of earthworks.

The stretch of blue sea, edged by the tumbling surf-beaten beach, and the uprising of foliage-covered hills, all brought out clearly by a tropical sun, formed a picture as far removed from the usual setting of war as could be. But war was there, and the scenery appealed to few. There was more interest in the drab hulls of the fleet and the outward reaching of the mighty guns.

That evening—the evening of June 3d—the "Yankee's" decks presented an animated spectacle. The novel surroundings and the prospect of action kept the boys interested. The "Rumor

Committee" was in active session, and one of its principal members, the captain's orderly, brought the news forward that the auxiliary cruiser would surely lead a procession of battleships into Santiago harbor the following day.

This was a little too strong for even the marines to swallow. We lay down by our loaded guns that night, feeling that it was well to be within easy reach of our defenders.

Hammocks were laid on the deck close to each five-inch breechloader, and the regular watch was doubled. Lack of experience made all these warlike preparations very impressive, and it was some time before the boys fell asleep. For my part, such a restlessness possessed me that, after trying to woo slumber for a half hour, I left my place and crawled over nearer the open port.

"Hello, Russ," whispered a voice, apparently from the outside. "Just lean out here if you want to cool off. Isn't the night air fine?"

A small figure wriggled in from where it had been hanging over the port sill, and in the faint light I recognized "Kid," as we called him, the smallest boy on board, and so pleasant and popular that we had unanimously elected him the mascot of the ship.

I was glad to see that it was "Kid." His

fund of ready wit and his never-failing good-nature made him a welcome companion at all times. He did not belong to my gun, being a "powder monkey" on No. 16, a six-pounder on the spar deck, but "Kid" was privileged, and he could have penetrated to the captain's cabin with impunity.

"Thought I'd drop down here for a rest," he began, stretching himself and yawning. "Too much tramping about on deck to sleep. Say, looks as if we were going to have a little rain, doesn't it?"

The moon had just passed behind a scurrying cloud, causing the silvery sparkle of its reflection to suddenly fade from the surface of the water. The lights and shadows on the nearby beach changed to a streaky dark smudge. There was a damp touch to the air.

"This would be a proper night for one of those sneaking torpedo boats to give us a scare," resumed "Kid," thoughtfully. "Funny ways of fighting those Dagoes have, eh? It's like prisoner's base that I played when I was a boy."

"Kid's" eighteen years were a mature age in his opinion.

"The two torpedo craft in Santiago harbor could do a great deal of damage if they were properly handled," I ventured. "They are magnificent vessels of their class. Look what Cushing did with a slow steam launch and a powder can on the end of a stick."

"The case was different."

"Yes, but——"

"Cushing was an American," interrupted the boy convincingly.

There was silence for awhile and we lolled in the port, gazing idly at the black spots in the gloom representing the blockading fleet. Between us and the shore was the "New Orleans," the faint tracery of her masts just showing above the distant background of the hills. The dampness in the air had increased, and a dash of rain came in the open port.

"What were you doing at the mast this morning, 'Kid'?" I asked by way of variety.

"Had a mustering shirt in the lucky bag."

I heard the boy chuckle. There was an escapade behind the remark.

"You know that wardroom Jap with the bad eye?"

"Yes."

"It was his shirt."

"But how——"

"It was this way. You know how hard it has been to put up with 'government straight' as a steady diet, don't you?"

I nodded. As "government straight" meant the extremely simple bill of fare provided by Uncle Sam, consisting of salt beef, pork, hardtack, beans, and canned butter, with an occasional taste of dried fruit, I was compelled to admit my acquaintance with it.

"Well, the other night I got to dreaming that I was back in New York," resumed "Kid." "I dreamt I dropped into a bang-up restaurant and ordered beefsteak, fried potatoes, pie, and——"

A groan came from one of the gun's crew, who was within hearing, and "Kid" lowered his voice.

"Hit him where he lived, I guess," he chuckled. "Well, I woke up so hungry that I couldn't stand it any longer. I looked up the Jap and struck him for a hand-out. He wanted a shirt, and I wanted something to eat, and we made a bargain. I brought him my extra mustering shirt—it was too large for me, anyway—and he gave me some bread and butter, cold potted tongue, three bananas, and——"

"For mercy's sake, stow that," muttered a voice from back of the gun-mount. "Don't we suffer enough?"

"That's 'Hand-Out' Hood," grinned "Kid." "He's kicking because he didn't get it. Well, I gave the shirt to the Jap, and what did he do

WE JOIN SAMPSON'S FLEET.

but lose it. My name was on the collar, and 'Jimmy Legs' put me on the report. The 'old man' was easy, though. Gave me four hours extra duty. I asked him if I couldn't work it out in the wardroom pantry."

"Kid's" chuckle came to a sudden stop, and he leaned out through the port.

"What's the matter?" I asked.

"Thought I saw something moving over there near the beach."

"Must have been a shadow."

"Guess so. Still, it looked like some kind of a——"

Bang!

The sharp report of a rapid-fire gun cut short his words. Another followed almost instantly, then came a regular volley. The effect on the crew of the "Yankee" was instantaneous. The men sleeping at the guns scrambled to their feet, hammocks were kicked out of the way, and before the word to go to general quarters was passed, every member of the crew was at his station.

"I thought I saw something moving inshore," cried "Kid," as he scurried away.

"It's a Spanish torpedo boat," muttered "Stump." "Great Scott! just listen to the 'New Orleans.' She's firing like a house afire."

Suddenly there came a deep, thunderous roar. It was the voice of a thirteen-inch gun on the "Massachusetts." Sixty seconds later the six-pounders on the "Yankee's" forecastle joined in the chorus, and the action became general.

"Do not fire without orders, men," cautioned Lieutenant Greene, the officer in charge of our division. "Just take it easy and bide your time."

It was our first experience in actual fighting, and our anxiety to "let loose" was almost overwhelming. We were held to our stations so rigidly that but few glimpses could be caught of the outside. The "New Orleans," on our starboard, was still rattling away.

Notwithstanding our own inaction (the gun deck battery was not used), there was a certain exhilaration in even listening to the sounds of conflict, and the eager, tense faces surrounding the guns reflected in the dim light of the deck lanterns such a fierce desire to fight that they were absolutely transfigured.

"Can't stand this much longer," muttered "Hay," the second captain, as a peculiarly vicious report came from the direction of the "Massachusetts." "Why don't they give a fellow a chance?"

"Steady, men," admonished Lieutenant

"THE SIX-POUNDERS ON THE 'YANKEE'S' FORECASTLE JOINED IN THE CHORUS" (*page* 112).

Greene. "Don't be impatient. Our turn will come soon. Steady!"

A turn of the hull—we were under way at half speed—brought the land on the port bow just then. The moon suddenly emerged from behind the clouds, and we who were nearest the port, distinctly saw a long, black object fade into the obscurity of the coast almost directly under Morro Castle.

"She's escaped!" groaned "Stump." "It's the torpedo boat, and she is safe again."

As if to prove the truth of his words the guns on the "New Orleans" and "Massachusetts" became silent; then word was sent below to "secure." Our first action was disappointing, but there was little grumbling. We knew full well that momentous events were bound to occur before long.

The following morning, shortly after daybreak, the torpedo boat "Porter" steamed alongside. Her coming created some excitement, and the "Yankee's" crew promptly lined the railing.

"What's that object on the deck?" asked "Stump," pointing to a long brass cylinder lying abaft the after conning tower.

"It's a torpedo, but not like those used in our navy," replied "Hay."

Captain Brownson leaned over the end of the bridge and waved his hand to Lieutenant Fremont, the "Porter's" commander. The latter was smiling, and as we watched, he made a gesture toward the mysterious brass cylinder.

"See that thing, Brownson?" he called out.
The captain nodded.
"It almost paid you a visit last night."
"What——"
"We picked it up near shore this morning and sunk another. That Spanish torpedo boat made a great attempt to sink one of our ships, and, if I am not mistaken, the 'Yankee' was her intended prey. Congratulations."

As the "Porter" steamed away we felt very much like congratulating ourselves. This was grim war of a certainty. Like the boy who was blown a mile in a cyclone without injury, we experienced a certain pride that we really had been in danger.

About the middle of the afternoon a signal was seen on the flagship. It was read at once, and immediately the boatswain's mate passed a call that sent a thrill of anticipation through us. It was:

"All hands clear ship for action!"

"CLEAR SHIP FOR ACTION!" (*page* 115).

CHAPTER IX.

CLEAR SHIP FOR ACTION.

The boatswain's mate's shrill piping and the long drawn out cry, "All hands clear ship for action!" was not entirely unexpected. An unusual activity on the part of the signal men on the flagship "New York" had not escaped our notice, and when the summons to prepare for battle echoed through the "Yankee's" decks it found us in readiness for prompt obedience.

At the time the call sounded a number of us were standing in the port waist idly watching the fleet and the shore. "Bill," a member of the powder division, whose father is a prominent real estate broker of New York, and whose great talent is for practical joking and general fun making, was telling a story. As we scattered at the summons, he started below with me. Even the circumstances could not prevent him following his hobby, and he whispered as we hurried along:

"Say, Russ, this reminds me of a good story

I once heard. There was a man who was too lazy to live and the neighbors finally decided to bury him. So they took him out to the village graveyard one morning before day and———"

"Here, you men, pass this mess chest below," interrupted an officer, beckoning to us. "Bill" grasped one end of the object indicated and lugged it to the hatch.

"They took the lazy man to the village graveyard, as I was saying," resumed "Bill," "and they buried him up to his neck in the earth. Then they hid back of tombstones and———"

"Less talking there, men," exclaimed the navigator, hurrying past us. "You 'heroes' do too much yarning to suit me. Get those things below at once. Shake it up."

"They are in an almighty hurry," grumbled "Bill." "The forts won't move. They'll be there to-morrow, I guess. Well, as I was saying, the villagers concealed themselves behind convenient tombstones and waited to see what the lazy man would do when he woke up. By and by day broke, and just as the sun gilded the windows of the old church the fellow who was buried up to his neck———"

"Chase those mess chests below, bullies," called out the boatswain's mate, dropping down the ladder a few feet away. "Lively there; the 'old man' wants to break a record. When you have finished, hustle to the oil and paint lockers and help carry all inflammable material to the spar deck."

For several minutes "Bill" worked away in silence. Between us we managed to lower a number of chests into the hold where they would be out of the way; then we disposed of more objects liable to produce unwelcome splinters, and finally we started toward the paint locker.

The gun deck presented a scene of the most intense activity. The process of clearing ship for action requires the united efforts of the entire crew. On vessels of the regular service, such as the "New York" or "Indiana," where everything has been constructed with a view to the needs of battle, the work is thoroughly systematized and comparatively easy. The "Yankee," being a merchant steamer hastily converted into a vessel of war, presented greater difficulties.

However, the crew was fairly familiar with its duties and the work progressed at a rapid rate. When "Bill" and I reached the paint locker we found several others preparing to convey the oil to the deck. It was a momentary respite, and "Bill" took advantage of it.

"When the sun rose the fellows hiding behind the tombstones saw the lazy man open his eyes," he resumed hurriedly. "He looked around and took in all the details of the scene, the old church with the windows glowing redly, the weeping willows shaking and trembling in the crisp morning breeze, the rows of sod-covered mounds, the crumbling tombstones, and on one side the old rickety fence marking the passing of the road. All this he saw and then——"

"Hear the news, fellows?" interrupted the "Kid," suddenly approaching. "We are going to—what's the matter, 'Bill'?"

For "Bill" had caught him by the slack of the shirt and one arm and was hustling him along the deck. The "Kid," looking aggrieved, went his way, and "Bill" returned.

"As I was saying," he continued calmly; "the lazy fellow saw all those things, then he threw back his head and laughed and laughed until the tears rolled down his cheeks. 'Whoop!' he cried, 'this is the best piece of luck I've struck yet. Hurray! blamed if it ain't the resurrection day and I'm the first feller above ground. Whoop!'"

After I had finished laughing I picked up a can of oil and asked:

"Where's the similarity, 'Bill'? It's a good story, but you said this reminded you of it."

"Humph! aren't we going to see the resurrection of some of these old Spanish fossils around here to-day?" "Bill" demanded. "And aren't we the first volunteer force on the spot? I guess that makes the story apropos."

As the "Yankee" was the first vessel manned by Naval Reserves to reach the scene of hostilities, I could not deny "Bill's" claim. Seeing the success of one story, he was on the point of telling another, when word came to hasten the clearing of the ship for action, and we were compelled to devote our energies to the work in hand.

The decks were sanded—a precaution that made more than one wonder if the spilling of blood was really anticipated; all boats and spare booms were covered with canvas to prevent the scattering of splinters, the steel hatch covers were closed down, hammocks were broken out of the racks and made to serve as an added protection to the forward wheel-house, and everything possible done to make the ship fit for action.

The time taken to gain this end did not exceed ten minutes, which was almost a record. Signals were displayed stating that we were in readiness, then all hands were called to general quarters. As we hurried to our stations I saw the entire blockading fleet moving slowly shoreward.

"We are going to bombard the Dagoes this trip for sure," observed the first captain of Number Eight as we lined up. "I see their finish."

"Don't be too sure," said "Stump." "There's many a slip between the muzzle and the target. Maybe we won't do much after all. Just to make it interesting I'll bet you a dinner at Del's that we will only chuck a bluff. What d'ye say?"

"Done, if you make it for the whole ship's company," chuckled the first captain.

"Stump" shook his head.

"A dinner at Del's for over two hundred hungry Reserves, and on a salary of $35 per month. Nope. Not on your life."

"Cast loose and provide," came the order.

There were a few moments of rapid work, then the battery was reported in readiness for firing. Through the open port we could catch a glimpse of the other vessels of the fleet, and the spectacle formed by the low-lying battleships, the massive cruisers, and the smaller, but equally defiant gunboats, was one long to be remembered.

Every ship was cleared for business. On the vessels of the "Oregon" class nothing could be seen but the gray steel of turrets and superstructure. The "New York" and the "Brooklyn" were similarly cleared. On the bridges could be seen groups of officers, but the decks were empty. Every man was at his gun.

The ships steamed in to within a short distance of the beach and then formed a semicircle, the heavier vessels taking the centre where they could directly face the forts. The little "Dolphin" was on the extreme right of the line, with the "Yankee" next.

When within easy range of the guns ashore there ensued a wait. No signal to fire came from the flagship, and there did not seem to be any move toward opening the battle by the forts. We stood at our guns in silence, awaiting the word, until finally patience ceased to be a virtue.

"Seems to me they ought to do something," murmured "Stump," glancing shoreward rather discontentedly. "Ain't we fair targets?"

"Why don't the admiral tell us to sail in?" queried the first captain in the same tone. "The day is fine and the range is good. There's the beggars plain enough with their measly old forts. What more is wanted?"

"Wish they would pipe down and light the smoking lamp," said the second loader. "It would be a great deal more fun than standing here like a dummy."

The sun had passed beyond the top of the hills, but the light was sufficiently strong to bring out in plain relief the batteries guarding the entrance to Santiago. Grim Morro Castle appeared almost deserted. The red and yellow banner of Spain flaunted lazily from the ramparts, but only here and there could be distinguished the little black dots representing the soldiers on guard. The earthworks and smaller forts were equally idle.

"We won't get anything out of them to-day," remarked "Stump" decisively. "It must be one of their eternal feast days when they won't even fight."

"There goes a signal on the flagship," exclaimed the first loader, pointing out the port. "I'll bet a dollar it's——"

"The signal to pull out again," groaned "Stump." "Didn't I say so?"

"The admiral intends to postpone the bombardment for some reason," I ventured. "Perhaps it's too late in the day."

Whatever the cause, it was now plain that we would not engage the forts. In obedience to the signals on the "New York," which were repeated by the "Brooklyn," the whole fleet returned to the former station several miles from shore. The word to "secure" was passed and presently the "Yankee" had resumed its former condition of armed watchfulness.

That evening after supper there was a gathering of the choice spirits of the crew in the vicinity of the after wheel-house. "Dye," the chief member of the "Yankee's" choir, started one of "Steve's" little songs, which, although rendered very quietly in deference to the rules observed on blockade, was greatly enjoyed. The air was "Tommy Atkins," and the words ran as follows:

> "They made us sign our papers for a year,
>   And dressed us in a natty sailor's suit;
>   They taught us how to heave the lead and steer,
>   And how to handle guns and how to shoot.
>   We fancied we'd be leaving right away
>   To capture prizes on the Spanish Main,
>   And be raising merry hades
>   With the dusky Spanish laddies,
>   And within a month come steaming home again.
>
> CHORUS.
>
> "But instead we ran a ferry
>   All along the Jersey shore,
>   And our tums were empty very,
>   And our hands were awful sore.
>   We would give our bottom dollar
>   Just to see a cable car,
>   Just to hear a newsboy holler,
>   Just to smoke a good cigar.
>
> "In times of peace we do not have to sweep
>   Or carry coal or stand on watch all night;

We do not have to scrub down decks or keep
    Our toothbrush chained, or brasswork shining
      bright.
We never washed our faces in a pail,
    We never heard the fog-horn's awful shriek,
      We never ate salt horse,
    We combed our hair, of course,
      And we never wore our stockings for a week."
CHORUS.

"Suppose you 'heroes' pipe down there," came from the darkness just then. "What do you think this is, a concert hall?"

"It's 'Cutlets,'" muttered "Stump." "He would like to make the ship a funeral barge."

We sat in silence for a while, watching the retreating form of the navigator passing forward; then Tom LeValley, a zealous member of Number Nine gun's crew, spoke up.

"Do you see those two lights twinkling over there about where the 'Dolphin' should be, fellows?" he asked.

Some one yawned and nodded.

"Reminds you of a story, eh?" asked "Bill," who was leaning against the rail. "Well, come to think of it I remember a———"

"Several years ago I happened to be a patient in a hospital over in Brooklyn," continued Tom. "I was almost well and about to leave the place when a man in the upper ward———"

"I had a cousin once who used to travel a great deal," interrupted "Bill," taking a seat on the deck with his back against a bitt. "One time he happened to be in a small town just outside of Dublin, Ireland. The inn was crowded and he had to take up his quarters with a family who occasionally rented out rooms. A circus and menagerie was giving exhibitions in the city, and one night the biggest monkey escaped from its cage and skipped out. They instituted a search at once, but the animal could not be found. Well, it happened that the family with whom my cousin was stopping consisted of father and mother and one son about ten years old. The boy, whose name was Mike, was a regular limb. Always in mischief and——"

"As I was saying," broke in Tom at this juncture, "when I was about to leave the hospital, a man in the upper ward concluded to depart this world for a better one. It happened about eight o'clock in the evening, and, as was usual in such cases, the nurse on watch was supposed to get several convalescent patients and a stretcher and carry the body down to a little wooden house a hundred yards from the main building. The nurse, with whom I was on friendly terms, had an important case to attend to just then and he asked me if I wouldn't take charge of the stretcher party. Well, we started down the yard, I leading the way with a lantern, and we finally reached the little house. We entered and——"

"Some people think they are the only story tellers in the group," remarked "Bill" with mild sarcasm at that interesting point. "To tell a good story with a point to it is an art. Now, as I was saying, this boy Mike would rather get into mischief than eat a—what's the Irish for potato?"

"Spud," suggested "Hod."

"Murphy," said "Stump."

"Well, it's immaterial. Anyway the boy was full of mischief. The night the monk got away he had been sent to bed early because of some trick he had played. He slept in a little room at the head of the stairs leading to the second story. His window opened on a lean-to shed, and, as it was a warm evening, the sash was raised. Shortly after the youngster got to bed, something slipped over the back fence, and after prowling about the yard for a moment, climbed upon the shed and through the window into the room where Mike was just in the act of falling asleep. The thing, which was about the youngster's size, crept over the floor toward the bed, and then with a spring, landed squarely upon——"

"Some people use more wind in telling a story than would fill a maintop-sail," drawled Tom. "There's nothing like getting at your subject. Now, when we reached the little wooden house we entered, and after accomplishing our errand, started back to the main building. While on the way it suddenly occurred to me that I had forgotten to close the door between the two rooms of which the house was composed. There was an open window in the front room, and there was no telling what might get in. I told the fellows to go on and I tasked back to the little house. I still carried the lantern, but just as I reached the door, it went out. I tell you, I felt like letting the whole thing go, but I didn't want to get the nurse into trouble. So I unlocked the front door, opened it, and, Great Scott! I saw——"

"There's everything in choosing a subject when you want to tell a good story," calmly interrupted Bill. "This story I am trying to tell has a laugh in it. You don't have to keep your hair down with both hands and feel the cold chills playing tag up and down your spinal column, like you have to do when some people are trying to yarn. Well, when the thing that had crept through the window landed on the bed, Mike let out a yell that could have been heard in Dublin. 'Ow-w-w!' he whooped, scrambling to the floor. He caught one sight of the visitor, and then made a dash for the window and slid clear to the ground, leaving pieces of shirt and his epidermis on every nail on the shed roof. The noise he made roused the father and mother below, and the latter started for the stairs. 'That b'ye 'll be the death av me yet,' she complained. 'I'll go up and give him a slap.' She lost no time in reaching the little room, and when she entered she saw the bed with what she thought was Mike under the clothes. 'Mike, ye rascal,' she exclaimed, 'turn down the sheet this minute. It's mesilf as 'll tache ye to raise a noise at this time o' night. For shame, ye spalpane! What, ye won't obey your own mother? I'll show ye. Take that!' She brought her hand down upon the figure outlined under the sheet with a resounding whack. The next second the thing leaped from the bed squarely into her arms. 'Wow! Murther! Mike, what have ye been doing?' she howled, adding at the top of her voice, 'Patrick, Patrick, come quick! The b'ye has got hold of your hair restorer. He's all covered with hair and he's gone daft. Murther!' With that the father made for the stairs as fast as his legs could carry him. Just as he got to the top——"

"The sight I saw when I opened the outer door of the little house almost knocked me silly," broke in Tom, rather excitedly. "There in the other room gleamed——"

"When Patrick reached the second floor," interrupted Bill, raising his voice, "he felt something strike him full in the chest; then two hairy arms clasped him about the throat and——"

"In the other room gleamed two——"

"Oh, give a fellow a chance, will you?" cried Bill. "You want the whole floor. What do you think——"

"Sh-h-h! here comes the executive officer," hastily whispered "Stump." "We've made too much racket. Let's go into the after wheelhouse."

"We must be quiet about it," spoke up the "Kid," warningly. "'Cutlets' is chasing around to-night, and if he catches us in there he'll raise Cain."

"All right," replied Bill. "And I'll finish that story if I have to stay up all night."

"Same here," retorted Tom, with evident determination. "Come on."

And we all followed the twain,

CHAPTER X.

WE BOMBARD SANTIAGO DE CUBA.

The after wheel-house on board the "Yankee" was a round structure of steel built on the spar deck directly over the counter. It contained a steering wheel to be used in case the wheel in the pilot-house should be disabled. When the chill winds of May and early June were blowing off the northern coast during the "Yankee's" period of cruising in that vicinity, the after wheel-house formed a snug and comfortable retreat for the men of the watch.

It was freely used for that purpose until the navigator chanced to discover the fact. He forthwith issued orders forbidding any person to enter the house, except on duty. His order, like many others, received respectful consideration—when he happened to be looking. In the present case we were so eager to hear the conclusion of the stories being related by the rival yarn-spinners, that we were fain to brave " Cutlets ' " displeasure. Led by Bill and Tom, we piled inside.

"What I was trying to say," spoke up the former, getting the first opening, "was that when Patrick reached the top of the stairs, something struck him full in the chest, and two hairy arms were thrown about his neck. The sudden shock sent him tumbling backward, and he fell kerflop! down the steps. Up above, his wife was howling to beat the band, 'Mike, Mike, ye spalpane! You do be killing your poor father. Och! why did I live to see this day?' In the meantime the real Mike—for the one inside was the escaped monk from the menagerie—had scooted for the police. They came, a half dozen of them, and as they entered the front door——"

"Time!" chuckled "Stump." "Give Tom a chance."

"As I opened the front door of the little wooden house where we had placed the body," said Tom, prompt to take advantage of the opportunity, "I saw two gleaming eyes glaring at me from the inner room. I tell you, my heart fell clean down into my boots."

"Should think it would," muttered the "Kid," peering about the wheel-house with a shiver. "Ugh!"

"I dropped the lantern," resumed Tom, "and staggered back. Just then a——"

"Half dozen policemen entered the front door just as Patrick and the supposed Mike reached the bottom of the stairs," broke in Bill, taking up the thread of his story. "Well, when the Irish coppers saw Pat with the monk hanging around his neck they thought the old Nick had him. They started to run, but the old woman reached the lower floor in time to see both Mike and the monkey. She grabbed a broom, but the monk slipped through the front door, and——"

"That's the end of your story. And a good job it is too," remarked Tom.

"It is better than having no end," retorted Bill. "You spin out a yarn to beat the band."

"It's getting late," spoke up "Hod," yawning. "If you fellows are going to chew the rag all night I——"

"Only a word more," interrupted Tom. "As I staggered back I fell into the arms of the nurse, who had come down to see what kept me. I explained in a hurry, and he lit a match. We both went in and discovered——"

"Sh-h-h! Get out of here, you fellows," suddenly spoke up a voice at the door on the starboard side. "Here comes 'Cutlets'!"

There was a scramble for the opposite door, and in much less time than is taken in the telling, the wheel-house was empty. We huddled in the shadows for a moment; then dodged forward. As we reached the hatch I heard the "Kid" ask Tom:

"Say, what was it you saw? Tell a fellow, won't you?"

"Two brass knobs on an old chest," was the calm reply.

"Huh!"

The following day being Sunday, was given over to rest and recreation and the writing of letters, until late in the afternoon. The day dawned clear but very warm. There was very little breeze stirring, and the spar and gun decks, where we spent the most of our time, were almost stifling. "Corking mats," as they are termed in naval parlance, were very much in evidence. The sailor's "corking mat" is a strip of canvas which he spreads upon the deck to protect his clothing from the tarry seams, when he feels the necessity for a siesta or nap, which is quite often.

Toward evening we were put to work at a task which gave welcome promise of coming action. Under the direction of the executive officer we broke out a number of bags of coal from the orlop deck and piled them five deep, and about the same number in height, around the steam steering engine under the forward wheel-house. This was to give added protection to a vital part of the ship.

The work was hard and unpleasant, especially to men who had not spent the major portion of their lives at manual labor, but it was one of those disagreeable fortunes of war to which we were growing accustomed, and we toiled without comment. That night when we turned in, that is, those who were fortunate enough to have the "off watch," it was generally rumored about the decks that the fleet would surely bombard early the following morning.

About two bells (five o'clock) the different guns' crews, who were sleeping at the batteries, were called by the boatswain's mates, and told to go to breakfast at once.

"It's coming," exclaimed "Hay," joyfully. "The old 'Yankee' will see her real baptism of fire to-day. 'Kid,' you young rat, you'll have a chance to dodge shells before you are many hours older."

"You may get a chance to stop one," retorted the boy.

After a hurried meal, word to clear ship for action was passed, and the "Yankee's" boys set

WE BOMBARD SANTIAGO DE CUBA.

to work with a vim. The task was done more thoroughly than usual. The boats and wooden hatches were covered with canvas, everything portable that would splinter was sent below, the decks were sanded, and all the inflammable oils were placed in a boat and set adrift for the "Justin," one of the colliers, to pick up.

The day seemed fitted for the work we had in hand. The sky was overcast, and occasionally a rain squall would sweep from the direction of the land, and envelop the fleet. It was not a cold, raw rain, like that encountered in more northern latitudes in early summer, but a dripping of moisture peculiarly grateful after the heat of the previous day.

Shortly before seven o'clock, the members of the crew were in readiness for business. The majority had removed their superfluous clothing, and it was a stirring sight to watch the different guns' crews, stripped to the waist and barefooted, standing at their stations. There was something in the cool, practical manner in which each man prepared for work that promised well, and it should be said to the everlasting credit of the Naval Reserves that they invariably fought with the calmness and precision of veterans whenever they were called upon.

In the present case, there would have been

some excuse for faint-heartedness. The crew of the "Yankee," made up of men whose previous lives had been those of absolute peace, who had never heard a shot fired in anger before their arrival at Santiago, who had left home and business in defence of the flag—these men went about their preparations for attacking the fortifications with as little apparent concern as if it were simply a yachting trip.

There was no holding back, no hesitancy, no looks of concern or anxiety, but when the signal to advance inshore appeared on the "New York," at six bells (seven o'clock), there was a feeling of relief that the time of waiting was over.

We were to be in it at last.

The flagship's signal to advance in formation was obeyed at once. Moving in double column, the fleet stood in toward the batteries. The first line, as we saw from the after port, was composed of the "Brooklyn," "Texas," "Massachusetts," and "Marblehead." The line to which the "Yankee" was attached, included, besides that vessel, the "New York," "Oregon," "Iowa," and "New Orleans." When within three thousand yards from shore, the first line turned toward the west, leaving us to steam in the opposite direction.

WE BOMBARD SANTIAGO DE CUBA.

The batteries ashore could now be plainly distinguished. Morro Castle, grim and defiant, seemed to ignore our coming, if the absence of life was any proof. Lower down on the other side of the entrance where the Estrella and Catalena batteries were located, there seemed to be more activity. Men could also be seen running about in some new batteries a little to the eastward of Morro Castle. It was evident to us at once that the enemy had not anticipated an attack on such a rainy, windy day.

On swept the two lines of ships without firing a shot until they formed a semicircle, with the heavier vessels directly facing the forts; then the "New York" opened fire with one of her heavy guns, the "Iowa" following immediately. At this moment, 7:45 a.m., the ships were arranged as follows, counting from the right: "New York," "Yankee," "New Orleans," "Massachusetts," "Oregon," "Iowa," "Indiana," "Texas," "Marblehead," and "Brooklyn." Guarding the extreme left were the "Vixen" and "Suwanee," and doing similar duty on the other flank were the "Dolphin" and "Porter."

The shot from the flagship was the signal for a general bombardment. There was no settled order of firing, but each ship just "pitched in," to use a common expression, and banged away at the forts with every available gun.

The scene on the gun deck of the "Yankee" was one never to be forgotten. When the word to commence firing reached us, we sprang to the work at once. Each crew paid strict attention to its own station, and the routine of loading and firing went on with the regularity of clockwork. A number of boxes of the fixed ammunition had been "whipped" up from below while we were steaming into position, and there was no lack of death-dealing food for the hungry maws of the battery.

Not much could be seen of the outside at first, as the task in hand claimed our strict attention, but after a while an occasional glimpse was obtained of the other ships and the forts. The heavy battleships, the "Indiana," "Oregon," "Massachusetts," "Iowa," and "Texas," were lost in the dense smoke of their guns. It was thrilling to see them, like moving clouds, emitting streams of fire which shot through the walls of vapor like flashes of lightning athwart a gloomy sky.

The noise was terrific. It seemed to gather at times in such an overwhelming, soul-stunning clamor of sound, that the very air was rent and split and shattered, and the senses refused

THE BOMBARDMENT OF MORRO CASTLE, SANTIAGO (*page* 138).

further burden. There was no possibility of hearing the human voice, save at odd intervals when a brief cessation occurred in the firing. Orders were transmitted by gestures.

The smoke was thick and stifling, the saltpetre fumes filling the throat and lungs, until breathing was difficult. The dense bank of vapor enveloping the ship also rendered it almost impossible to aim with any accuracy. We of Number Eight gun were early impressed with this fact, and "Hay," the second captain, exclaimed during a lull:

"It's that fellow in charge of Number Six. He won't give us any show. Just look how he's working his crew. Did you ever see the beat of it?"

The captain of Number Six, a broker of considerable note in New York, a member of the Calumet Club, and the son of a distinguished captain in the Confederate navy, was fighting his gun with savage energy. Under his direction, and inspired by a running fire of comments from him, the different members of Number Six crew were literally pouring a hail of steel upon the batteries. The firing was so rapid, in fact, that it kept our port completely filled with smoke, much to our sorrow.

Notwithstanding that fact, "Hay," the second

captain of Number Eight, did such marvellous shooting, that word presently came from Captain Brownson on the bridge, publicly commending him. We were correspondingly elated, and worked all the harder.

It was not until we had been firing some time that we began to take particular note of our surroundings. At first the novelty of the situation and a state of excitement, natural under the circumstances, kept us absorbed in our duties, but when it became apparent that the engagement was to be a matter of hours—and also that the Spaniards did not aim very well—we commenced to look about.

One of the first things to strike me personally, and it was rather humorous, was the appearance of "Stump," the second loader. Orders had early been given to avoid exposing ourselves to the enemy's fire as much as possible. "Stump," than whom no more daring and aggressive man could be found on board, thought it wise to obey, so he crouched behind the gun-mount and compressed himself so as to be out of range. From this position he had only to reach out one hand to train the gun, which was his special duty. Meanwhile, he continually urged "Hay" to keep on firing.

"Doesn't make any difference whether you can see or not," he exclaimed. "Shoot anyway. Give it to the beggars! That's the ticket, old chap. Now another. Whoop! did you see that land? Ah-h-h! we are the people."

As the novelty of the scene gradually wore off we began to enjoy it hugely. We pumped away at the guns, commenting freely on the enemy's marksmanship. We felt more like a party watching a fireworks display than the crew of a warship engaged in bombarding a number of forts.

The two lines were steaming back and forth in front of the batteries, firing as the guns would bear. At first, Morro Castle and the smaller forts maintained a spirited fire, but finally their response to our fusillade slackened considerably, and it became evident that they had been driven from their guns.

The difference in aim between the Spanish gunners and ours was very perceptible. Their shells invariably passed over the ships or landed short, and at no time during the engagement were any of the American vessels in imminent danger. This was not due to length of range either, as the lines were maintained at from two to four thousand yards. As Bill put it, " Any Dago that can't hit a flock of barn doors like this fleet, had better go back home and hoe onions."

The ships of our fleet also made better targets than did the batteries ashore. It was certainly easy to distinguish the position of each vessel, but as the Spanish batteries were nearly all situated a short distance back from the crest of the ridge with a background little different in color from that of the battery, we found it difficult to locate them at times. Our elevation had to be perfect, as with an inch or two below or above, the projectile would either vanish in the distance or take effect on the cliffs below the batteries.

We of Number Eight gun, when the "Yankee" was steaming with the starboard broadside bearing, managed to slip across the deck and watch the firing from the ports and deadlights. It was really beautiful to see the landing of the great shells upon the forts and surrounding earth. Some battered into the soft spots on the cliffs, sending huge masses of dirt and débris high into the air; then when the explosion came, there would follow a great cloud of dust resembling the wavering smoke over a city fire.

Others struck the harder portions of the cliff, bursting into a shower of fragments, each kicking up its own pother of dirt and shattered rock. At times a shell would land in a crack in the face of the hill, and immediately following would come an upheaval of stones. These boulders, many of them of immense size, would roll down the slope and splash in the water at the base, creating a series of fountain-like cascades.

Accompanying the display was a continuous roar of explosion and detonation that echoed and reëchoed across the water like the pealing of tropical thunder. In fact, it was these noises, mingled with the fierce reports of our guns, which impressed us the most. Taking it all in all, the scene was spectacular in the extreme.

"Boys," remarked No. 7 of our crew—"Morrie," we called him—"this sight is worth all the coaling and standing watches and poor food we have had to put up with. I would experience it all over again just to see this bombardment."

And we heartily agreed with him.

After a time it seemed as if the admiral was determined to plump shells into the vicinity of Santiago until there was nothing left to fire at. There had been a continuous outpouring of projectiles from the guns of the fleet for over an hour, yet that grim line of gray steel fortresses still passed and repassed in front of the forts.

It was really growing monotonous, when

something occurred at the gun to which I was attached that served to give us an exciting minute or two. "Hay" had just fired a shot which caught one of the new batteries directly in the centre. The shell was extracted, and another inserted, but when the second captain pressed the electric firing lanyard, there was no report. The shell had missed fire.

In an instant we recalled the fate of the unfortunate marine corporal, and we eyed each other with something like consternation. It was necessary to extract the defective cartridge, and the action would certainly be accompanied with grave peril.

We turned to "Stump." The disagreeable duty was his.

"It's got to be done, fellows," he said, steadily enough. "The cartridge must come out some time. Stand back there and I'll——"

"Wait a moment," interrupted the officer of the division. "We will see if it can't be done without much risk. Bring a rope, one of you."

The required article was brought in a hurry. The bombardment was now at its height, and the thunderous roaring of the guns was increasing with every passing second. Above and around us the vicious reports of the "Yankee's" five-inch rapid-firers seemed like one continuous volley. A hoarse cheer came from a nearby ship, proclaiming the landing of some favored shot.

"Hurry, fellows," shouted "Hay" in an ecstasy of impatience. "Lively there; we're missing all the sport."

CHAPTER XI.

A PERILOUS MOMENT.

The scene on the gun deck of the "Yankee" at that moment would have made an eloquent subject for the brush of a Meissonier. It was the deck of a warship in battle, and the spectacle enacted was accompanied by an orchestra of the mighty guns of a fleet in action.

Imagine a compartment of steel, a compartment filled with smoke that surged and eddied as the ship lunged forward or rolled upon a heavy swell.

Imagine scattered about in this pungent vapor many groups of men, men half-naked, perspiring; their glistening bodies smeared and stained with the grime of conflict.

Imagine in the centre of one of these groups a wicked, menacing gun—a five-inch breech-loader, its long, lean barrel raised shoulder-high upon the apex of a conical gun-mount, near the base of which are significant wooden cases, some empty and others filled with elongated, formi-

A PERILOUS MOMENT.

dable cartridges; and pails of black, dirty water ascum with powder; and other objects each significant of war.

Imagine these things, and then understand that this gun, made to be turned against an enemy, has now turned against its workers. In the bore, pent in by the polished breechblock, is a cartridge which has failed in its duty. It is apparently defective.

The tide of battle is surging on; other ships of the bombarding fleet are still pouring their shot and shell upon the grim array of forts ashore; other guns of this ship are pursuing their duty with savage energy. But this gun is silent.

The men wax impatient. It is the height of the conflict. Many shots have been fired, and many more will yet be required to subdue the enemy. To be "out of action" will mean passiveness in the face of the enemy. Anything but that.

There is a rivalry between the guns' crews. It is a rivalry as to which shall make the best shots and create the most damage. The members of Number Eight—the after gun on the port side—are proud of their record. Their second captain—he whom they call "Hay"—has received the public commendation of the captain himself, sent down from the bridge in the midst of the battle. It is a mark of distinction not given freely, and Number Eight is eager for more honors.

But the men have not forgotten a similar case, occurring on the voyage down the coast, when another cartridge failed, and on being extracted from the breech chamber, exploded, killing a marine corporal and wounding others.

The men of Number Eight have not forgotten that tragedy, and that is why their gun is now to them a menacing creature of steel, whose breath may be the breath of death. They stand in groups, they eye it, they speculate, and they feel that a desperate and perilous duty is before them.

The risk must be taken. The cartridge must be extracted. It is a fortune of war which all who enlist must expect. But it is one thing to fall before an enemy's blow, and another to lose your life at the stroke of your own weapon.

The officer of the division steps forward.

"We will see if we can't take it out without much danger," he says, briefly. "Bring a rope."

One is hastily procured, and the first captain —a great, brawny, good-natured fellow, who has spent years at sea—deftly fastens the bight of the rope to the handle of the breechblock. He then retreats a short distance and signifies his readiness.

"When I give the word," calls out the officer, "pull handsomely. Ready—pull away!"

From out the smoke-filled compartment men lean forward, eagerly—anxiously. They instinctively shrink back as the breech plug slowly moves. Then, when it finally opens, revealing the brass head of the cartridge inside the firing chamber, a sigh of relief comes from all.

But the danger is not yet over.

The defective projectile must be taken out and tossed into the sea. The second loader steps forward at a signal from the gun captain. This second loader is "Stump." He shows no fear, but draws out the heavy cartridge, handling it as he would a harmless dummy, and passes it to another man and myself. Carrying it between us—and carrying it gingerly—we hasten to the side, and with a powerful swing, launch the hundred-pound projectile through the open port.

It barely clears the port sill, coming so close to it, in fact, that for one breathless second we think that it will strike. As the shell passes from view, another sigh of relief comes from the spectators. "Hay" passes a grimy towel over his perspiring face.

"Whew! that was a ticklish moment," he said, solemnly. "I'd just as soon not handle any more defective shells."

Which exactly represented our sentiments.

Three minutes later Number Eight was barking away at the forts ashore, and the episode of the cartridge that missed fire was a thing of the past.

The bombardment of Santiago had now lasted over an hour. As yet not one of the American vessels had been reached by a shell, nor had the forts suffered any perceptible damage. The fleet, roaring and thundering, was swinging back and forth through the great semicircle, the smoke from the guns was banking along the beach, and from Morro Castle and its attending batteries came sharp, defiant answers to the interminable volleys fired by our squadron.

"It's a good thing Uncle Sam's shot locker is pretty capacious," remarked Flagg, as we shoved another cartridge into the yawning breech of our five-inch gun. "If we haven't fired over three hundred rounds since seven o'clock I can't count."

"It'll be double that before we get through," grunted "Long Tommy," as we stepped back from the loaded gun. "Steady, there. Stand by!"

A PERILOUS MOMENT.

A motion to "Hay," who held the firing lanyard, and almost instantly came the sharp, vicious report of the breechloader. Each man sprang back to his station, and the process of reloading went on without delay. The battle smoke from Number Six, which had filled our port for some time, cleared away just then, enabling us to see "Hay's" last shot strike squarely upon the outer line of earthworks of the Punta Gorda battery.

"Splendid shot, 'Hay'!" exclaimed our division officer, briefly.

"Bully, that's what it is—bully!" cried "Stump," patting the second captain upon the back.

"Hurray! it's knocked out a gun," reported "Dye," from nearer the port. "I saw the piece keel over backward."

There was no time for further comment. When a gun's crew is firing at will, and the excitement of combat has taken possession of the individual members, the task in hand requires all one's attention. We of Number Eight had suffered one delay, and we really felt that the lost time must be made up.

Personal impressions in battle have been described in prose and poem until the subject is hackneyed, but it may be of interest to note that the impressions experienced by the novices in naval warfare manning the "Yankee," during the bombardment of Santiago, consisted mainly of one feeling. It was well-voiced by "Hod," who said many days later:

"I felt just as I did one time when I attended Barnum's circus in Madison Square Garden. They had three rings, two platforms, a lot of tight-ropes and trapezes and other things all going at the same time. Before I had been in the place three minutes I was wishing for a hundred eyes. And that is the way I felt at Santiago."

What we saw of the bombardment was limited to the range of our gun port, but that little was worth all the hardships and toil and discomforts of the whole cruise. The spectacle of the fleet itself was almost enough. To see the great ships ploughing through the water, each enveloped in a shroud of smoke, shot here and there with tinges of ruddy flame; to see that mighty line swinging and swaying in front of the enemy; to see the shells land and explode in fort and battery; to see the great gaps torn in cliff and earthworks; to see the geyser-like fountains of water spout up here and there as the Spanish shells struck the surface of the bay—to see all this, and to hear the accompanying thunder and boom-

ON THE GUN DECK DURING THE BOMBARDMENT (*page* 152).

A PERILOUS MOMENT.

ing of the guns, was payment in full for coal handling and standing watch and "Government straight." Not one of the "Yankee" boys would have missed the spectacle for anything earth could offer.

During the second hour of the attack we were enabled to observe the work being done by other vessels of the fleet. Near us was the gallant "New Orleans," the ship purchased from Brazil. Her foreign build made it easy to distinguish her, and, as she was the only craft using smokeless powder, she presented a prominent mark. The guns on board the "New Orleans" were being served rapidly and with precision, and we saw a number of shots strike well within the limits of the batteries.

At our end of the line the flagship "New York," the "Iowa," and the "Oregon" were pouring an appalling fire into some new earthworks near Morro Castle. It was seen that but very few shots were sent in the direction of the latter, and it transpired that Admiral Sampson had issued strict orders to the fleet to avoid endangering Lieutenant Hobson and his brave companions, who were supposed to be imprisoned in old Morro. Before the end of the second hour the "New York" and the "New Orleans" had succeeded in completely silencing

Cayo Battery, dismantling the guns and wrecking the outer fortifications.

At the other end of the line Admiral Schley's division was doing splendid work. We could see the "Massachusetts," "Brooklyn," and "Texas" move in toward shore and open fire at close range. It was a stirring sight, this mighty duel between warships and forts. As compared with the cliffs and hills of the land, the ships seemed veritable pigmies, but in this strife the pigmies were all powerful.

The guns of the fleet were working havoc in the forts ashore, and we could see the Spanish artillerymen abandon battery after battery. Cayo, Punta Gorda, Estrella, and Catalena were rapidly being vacated. The former was entirely out of the fight, and the others were replying only at intervals. Presently the "Massachusetts" and "Marblehead" advanced within two thousand yards of the Estrella fortification and began such a terrific firing that within a few minutes a great cloud of smoke appeared above the works. The Spanish guns became quiet at once, and a rousing cheer went up from the fleet.

"Hay," in his exuberance, wanted to send a five-inch shell from our gun at the burning fort, but the distance was too great and he was compelled to be content with a couple of well-aimed shots at the nearest battery.

"I wish we had thirteen-inch guns and the range was about ten feet," grumbled "Stump." "I'd like to smash the whole outfit in a pair of minutes. By Cricky! we have poured enough good old American steel into those forts to build a bridge across the Atlantic, but the dagoes are still giving us guff."

"It won't last much longer," said Tommy reassuringly. "From the looks of those batteries they haven't much fight left. I'll bet a hardtack against a prune we haul off at four bells."

"Licked?" queried Flagg.

"Nope."

"Will the Spaniards give up?" asked "Dye."

Tommy hesitated before replying. It was a brief lull and we were resting at the gun. The crew, grimy, dirty, battle-stained and tired, was glad to lean against the side of the deck or a convenient stanchion. Tommy's long service in the regular navy as apprentice and seaman made his opinions official, and we were always glad to listen to his explanations.

"Will the Spaniards give up?" repeated "Dye."

"Yes, and no," replied the first captain thoughtfully. "You see, it's this way. Those dagoes are not fools by any means. They have selected good places for their batteries, and they know earthworks are hard to destroy. They aren't like the old-style stone forts that could be knocked to pieces in no time. When a shell, even a thirteen-incher, hits a mound of earth it tears up the dirt and spoils the look of the parapet, but it really doesn't do much harm. To completely ruin an earthwork battery, you must dismantle every gun in it. And that's pretty hard to do. Mark my words, those fellows will give us a shot of defiance after we quit."

"What's the idea of all this bombarding then?" asked "Stump." "We'd be much better 'caulking off,' seems to me."

"And think what it costs the Government," I suggested. "The cost of the projectiles and the wear and tear to guns and ships must be something enormous."

Tommy's answer was drowned in the thundering roar of the "New York's" battery, which opened fire just then a short distance away, but it was evident he agreed with me. A moment later Number Eight went into action once more, and we worked the breechloader without cessation until the conclusion of the bombardment, which came a half hour later.

The fortifications ashore had entirely ceased

firing, and at ten o'clock a signal to stop bombarding appeared on the flagship. It was obeyed with reluctance, and it was evident the crews of the various ships were anxious and eager to continue. As the fleet drew off there was a puff of smoke in one corner of Punta Gorda battery and a shell whizzed over the "Massachusetts." A second shot came from one of the earthworks, and still another from Punta Gorda; then the firing ceased again.

"Didn't I tell you so?" quietly remarked Tommy. "The beggars ain't licked yet."

"But they got a taste of Uncle Sam's strength," said Flagg.

"And I'll bet anything they haven't enough whole guns left to equip one small fort," added "Stump."

"I heard the skipper say the destruction of life must be enormous," spoke up the "Kid," stopping on his way aft to deliver a message. "He watched the whole thing with his glass. He told 'Mother Hubbub' the moral effect was worth all the trouble."

"That's an expert opinion," observed "Hay," wiping off the breech of the gun. "Now you've had your little say, youngster, so just trot along."

The fleet presently reached its former station

several miles off shore, and the bombardment of Santiago was at an end.

No attempt was made to clean ship until late in the afternoon. The men were permitted to lie around decks and rest, smoke, and discuss the fight, which they did with exceeding interest. When dinner was piped at noon, the shrill call of the boatswain's whistle was welcome music. A sea battle is a good appetizer.

About four o'clock in the afternoon the fleet was treated to a spectacle both novel and humorous. The little "Dolphin," a gunboat of not fifteen hundred tons displacement, which was keeping guard close in shore, began to use her guns. A battery near the channel returned the fire, but the plucky little craft maintained her position, and from the series of rapid reports coming from her four-inch breechloaders and six-pounders, it was evident she had something important on hand.

The "Yankee" was signalled to run in to her assistance, but before we could reach a position, the "Dolphin" had accomplished her task. It was not until then that we discovered what she had been doing.

"May I never see home again if the gunboat hasn't corralled a railway train in a cut!" exclaimed "Patt." "Just look there, fellows.

A PERILOUS MOMENT.

See that ridge of earth on the other side of the channel? Just under it is a track running into a cut and——"

"The 'Dolphin' has closed up both ends," interrupted "Stump," with a laugh. "She's knocked down a pile of earth and débris on the track and the train can't get out. What a bully trick."

Flagg produced a glass, and after a careful scrutiny reported that he could see part of the train lying on its side at the eastern end of the cut. He could also distinguish a number of bodies, and it was plain that the Spanish loss had been heavy. It was not until later that we learned the details, which were as follows:

After the bombardment the "Dolphin" remained at her station, firing occasionally at the batteries ashore. She was directly opposite a cut in the cliff, through which runs a little railway connecting the iron mines with the dock in Santiago harbor. During the bombardment, a train loaded with Spanish troops remained in the cut, and at its conclusion attempted to leave. It was espied by the "Dolphin" and driven back. It tried the other end with like results, and for an hour this game of hide-and-seek was kept up, to the discomfiture of the train. While waiting for the train to appear at either end, the gallant little gunboat shelled a small blockhouse, and in time disabled it. Then she steamed back to the fleet and reported that she had " wrecked a trainload of troops and dismantled a blockhouse." When she left for her station again she was applauded by the whole squadron. We learned later that one hundred and fifty men were killed on the train.

Shortly after supper the " Yankee's " whaleboat was called away and sent to the flagship, returning an hour later with sealed orders from the admiral.

At midnight we quietly steamed from our station and passed out to sea, our destination being unknown to all save the commanding officer.

CHAPTER XII.

IN SEARCH OF ADVENTURE.

When a man-of-war sails from port under what are called "sealed orders," which means that the orders given to the captain by the admiral are not to be opened for a certain number of hours, or until the ship reaches a certain degree of latitude, there is a mystery about the affair which appeals strongly to the crew.

We of the "Yankee" felt very curious as to our destination when we left Santiago that night, and the interest was greatly stimulated by the discovery, before we had gone very far, that the "St. Louis" and "Marblehead" were following us.

The "Rumor Committee" went into active session without delay.

"Bet I can guess it," said "Stump," as a half dozen of us met in the gangway. "We are bound for a cable station somewhere."

"To cable the news of the fight?" said Flagg.

"No. That was done by one of the other ships."

"What then?"

"To get permission from Washington to go ashore and reclaim all that steel we wasted in the bombardment."

There was a laugh at this sally.

"I have been figuring on the cost of the fight," remarked "Hay," after a pause. "A five-inch shell is worth $60, and as we fired about two hundred and fifty, it means just $15,000 worth of five-inchers alone."

"Then there are the six-pounders."

"They cost $20 a shot," resumed "Hay," reflectively. "I guess we must have fired about a million of them."

"Hardly that," smiled Tommy, "but we expended enough to bring the total up to $18,000 at the very least. War is a costly thing, boys."

When the quartermaster on duty came off watch he joined us in the gangway, and reported that we were steering a straight course to the southward.

"If we keep it up we'll land somewhere near the Antarctic Ocean," remarked Kennedy, doubtfully. "I wonder——"

"I know, I know," broke in the "Kid," eagerly. "We're going for ice."

The burning question was solved at daybreak. The morning sun brought into view a stretch of highland which proved to be Cuba. We had steamed out to sea on scouting duty, and had doubled on our tracks, as it were. The port we found to be Guantanamo, a small place some forty miles to the eastward of Santiago.

The town itself lies on a bay connected with the sea by a tortuous and winding channel. The entrance is protected by a fort and several blockhouses, and when we steamed inshore we espied the "St. Louis" and "Marblehead" laying to, waiting for us outside.

The "Marblehead" preceding us, we entered the harbor, and the two ships began a lively bombardment, while the "St. Louis" lay outside. Shortly after the firing began, a Spanish gunboat was seen steaming out past the fort. A few shots in her direction sent her scurrying back again, and that was the last seen of her during the fight. After the battle of the previous day, this affair seemed insignificant, and aroused little interest.

The blockhouses were destroyed and the fort silenced after a short period of firing, and the "St. Louis" proceeded with the duty which evidently had caused our visit. It was the cutting of a cable connecting Guantanamo with the outer world.

Our little fleet steamed to sea in the afternoon, returning just before dark. The fort, showing signs of reanimation, was treated to another bombardment, which effectually settled it. A small fishing hamlet composed of a dozen flimsy huts of bamboo was set on fire and burned to the ground. When we left Guantanamo shortly after dark, bound back for Santiago, we had the satisfaction of knowing that one more blow had been struck against Spanish rule in the fair isle of Cuba.

At dawn the following day, Santiago was sighted. The fleet was still lying off the entrance like a group of huge gray cats watching a mouse hole. As we passed in, the flagship began signalling, and it soon became noised about the ship that we had received orders to leave for Mole St. Nicholas after dark.

"It looks as if the 'Yankee' will come in handy as a messenger boy," said "Stump." "When the admiral wants 'any old thing' he tells his flag officer to send the Naval Reserve ship."

"It's a good thing to be appreciated," grinned "Dye." "To tell the truth, though, I'd rather be on the move than lying here watching the land."

IN SEARCH OF ADVENTURE.

"We don't want to be away when Cervera comes out," remarked Flagg.

"When he comes out," retorted "Stump," emphasizing the first word meaningly. "The old gentleman knows when he is well off and he'll stay inside."

"Which, as the Texan said when he was accused of stealing a horse," put in Tommy, "remains to be proved. Just you keep your eye on the gun and wait."

"There goes another string of signals on the 'New York,'" exclaimed "Dye," pointing toward the flagship. "Whiz! I'd hate to be a signalman aboard of her. They are always at it."

The flagship of a fleet like that assembled in front of Santiago during the blockade, is certainly kept very busy. In the naval service, everything in the way of routine emanates from the flagship. Every ship in the squadron, for instance, takes the uniform of the day from her. The number of sick each morning must be reported by signal; all orders (and they are legion) are transmitted by wigwag or bunting; scores of questions are asked daily by each ship, and it is indeed seldom that the signal yards of a flagship are bare of colored flags.

In the American navy the present methods of

communication are by the use of flags representing numerals, by the Meyer code of wigwag signals, and by a system of colored electric bulbs suspended in the rigging. The latter system is called after its inventor, Ardois.

In the daytime, when ships are within easy distance, wigwagging is commonly used. A small flag attached to a staff is held by the signalman in such a position that it can be seen by the ship addressed. A code similar to the Morse telegraph alphabet is employed. By this system the flag, when waved to the right, represents 1, or a dot; and 2, or a dash, when inclined to the left. Each word is concluded by bringing the flag directly to the front, which motion is called 3. Naval signalmen, generally apprentices, become very expert, and the rapidity with which they can wigwag sentences is really remarkable.

The Ardois system of night signalling consists of electric lights attached to the rigging. There are four groups of double lamps, the two lamps in each group showing red and white respectively. By the combination of these lights letters can be formed, and so, letter by letter, a word, and thence an order, can be spelled out for the guidance of the ships of a squadron. The lamps are worked by a keyboard generally placed on the upper bridge.

The "flag hoist" system, as it is termed, consists of the displaying of different flags at some conspicuous place like the masthead. There are a great many flags and pennants, differing in color, shape, and design, each having its own particular meaning, and when three or four are shown aloft together, a number is formed, the significance of which can only be determined by referring to a code book. Each navy has a private code, which is guarded with great care. So particular are Governments in this respect, that the commanding officer of every ship has instructions to go to any length to destroy the code book, if capture is imminent. During the late war with Spain it was reported at one time that the Spanish code had been secured. This means that the Dons will be compelled to adopt an entirely new code of signals.

Besides the above systems, signalling in the navy includes various other devices. For instance, the fog whistle can be utilized in connection with the Meyer system of numerals. One toot represents 1, two short toots 2, and a long blast the end of a word. In a fog, this is the only means practicable. Similar sounds can be made by horn or gunfire. At night searchlights are often used by waving the beam from the right to the left, thus forming an electric wigwag, or by flash like the heliograph. On small ships not fitted up with the Ardois system, the Very night signal is used. This consists of a pistol made for the purpose, which discharges lights similar to those found in the ordinary Roman candles. The colors are red and green, and they are fired in combinations expressing the numbers from 1 to 9 and 0, so that the numbers to four digits contained in the signal book may be displayed.

The "Yankee" was rigged with the Ardois lamps, and she also carried all the necessary signal flags and other paraphernalia required to communicate with other vessels of the fleet. The signalmen on board had been drilled in their work as members of the Naval Reserve prior to the beginning of the war, and they were experts to a man.

On the evening of June 8th, while we were idling about decks awaiting the order to get under way, a small boat came alongside, having as a passenger a captain of the army. He proved to be a special agent who had succeeded in visiting the vicinity of Santiago, and was on his way to Mole St. Nicholas for the purpose of cabling to Washington. The mysterious manner in which he boarded the ship, and the quickness with which we steamed from port, created some excitement, and we felt the importance of our mission.

The night was dark and muggy—an ideal time for torpedo-boat work, and extra lookouts were posted by order of the captain. Nothing of interest occurred, however, until early next morning. The ship was ploughing along at a steady gait, and those of the watch who were not on actual duty were snatching what sleep they could in out-of-the-way corners, when suddenly the call to "general quarters" was sounded. Long practice caused prompt obedience, and the various guns' crews were soon ready for action.

Very few of us knew just what was on foot until the "Kid," in passing, contrived to convey the interesting information that a big Spanish fleet had been sighted dead ahead.

"That's funny," remarked "Stump," trying to peer from the port. "We are not changing our course any. Surely the 'old man' doesn't intend to tackle them alone."

"I guess the 'Kid' is 'stringing' us," observed Tommy, sagely. "He's up to that trick every time. We're not chasing Spanish fleets alone. The captain knows his business all right, all right."

Word was brought from the upper deck presently, that we were in pursuit of a strange steamer which had been discovered lurking on the horizon. She failed to respond to our signals, and chase was made forthwith. The "Yankee's" speed soon proved superior to that of the stranger, and within an hour we had her close aboard.

"It's an English tramp from the looks of her," reported "Hay," who had a choice position near the gun port. "She's got a dozen people on the bridge and they are badly scared."

A blank six-pounder was fired, but she did not heed it, so a shot was fired across the stranger's bows, and she hove-to in short order.

"Steamer ahoy!" came faintly to our ears from on deck. "What steamer is that?"

The answer reached us in disjointed sentences, but we heard enough to set us laughing. Tommy smacked his hand upon the breech of the gun and chuckled: "It's one of those everlasting press boats. The sea is full of 'em."

"What in the deuce did they run for, I wonder?" exclaimed Kennedy.

"Afraid of us, I suppose. It's ticklish times around here, and I don't blame them. Press boats are not made to fight, you know."

"That idea doesn't carry out their motto," drawled "Dye."

"How's that?" asked Flagg, innocently.

"Why, they claim that the pen is mightier than the sword, don't they?"

After the laugh had subsided, "Morrie," one of the Rochester detail, who acted as a shellman in the crew of Number Eight, said seriously:

"I am a great admirer of the press representatives down here, fellows. They are capable, good writers, and there is not a branch of the whole outfit that has been more faithful to duty. They were sent here to get the news, and they get it every time. There has never been a war more ably reported than this, and, although the correspondents have to hustle day and night, they still find time to keep us informed, and to give us an occasional paper from home. They are good fellows all."

"Amen!" said "Hay."

After a time, the press boat sheered off, and we continued on our course. Later in the morning another steamer was sighted. The "Yankee" was sent after her at full speed. The chase crowded on all steam, but she was soon overhauled, and found to be a Norwegian trader. After a satisfactory explanation she was permitted to go. Three hours later the "Yankee" dropped anchor off Mole St. Nicholas, a Haytian seaport brought into some prominence through the location of a cable station.

Mole St. Nicholas is a little collection of tropical-looking houses set among palm trees at the foot of a large hill, which in places aspires to the dignity of a mountain. The town itself is rather picturesquely situated, the foliage-covered background and beautiful inlet of pure clear water giving it a natural setting very attractive to our eyes.

After we had been anchored an hour or so, a bumboat came out, manned by a crew of two coal-black negroes who spoke a French patois, intermingled with comical English. The boat itself was a queer, stubby craft propelled by home-made oars. Before the morning was well advanced the ship was surrounded by boats carrying shells, limes, prickly pears, green cocoanuts, bananas, fish, and " water monkeys." The latter were jugs made of a porous clay, and they were eagerly purchased. The " water monkey " is a natural cooler, and when placed in a draught of air will keep water at a temperature delightful in a warm latitude.

We parted with our mysterious passenger, the army officer, and weighed anchor just as the sun was setting. Lookouts were posted early, and special instruction given by the captain to maintain a vigilant watch. The fact that we were in the very theatre of war, and that several Spanish cruisers, including the Spanish torpedo boat "Terror," were reported as being in the vicinity, kept a number of us on deck.

"It is one thing lying off a port with a lot of other ships and bombarding a few measly earthworks, and another to be sneaking about in the darkness like this, not knowing when you will run your nose against an enemy twice as large," said Flagg, as several of Number Eight's crew met on the forecastle. "I tell you, it feels like war."

"Reminds me of a story I heard once," put in "Stump," lazily. He was lounging over the rail with his back to us and his words came faintly. The deck was shrouded in gloom, and the vague outlines of the pilot-house, only a dozen feet away, was the length of our vision aft. A soft, purling sound came from over the side where the waves lapped against the steel hull. A shovel grated stridently now and then in the fire room, and occasionally a block rattled or a halliard flapped against the foremast overhead. The surroundings and the strange, weird "feel" of the darkness were peculiarly impressive.

"I don't know whether we care to hear any story," observed "Hay." "Better keep it until later, 'Stump.' The night's too wonderful to do anything except lounge around and think. Whew! isn't it dark?"

"This story I was going to tell you requires a setting like this," replied "Stump." "It is about a ship that started from England years and years ago. She had as passengers a lot of lunatics who were to be experimented upon by a doctor about as crazy as they. He bought the ship, fitted it up with a number of little iron cages, and set forth with his queer cargo. Ten days out, the lunatics broke from their quarters and captured the vessel. One of them, who had been a sea captain in his time, took charge, and proceeded to carry out a little idea of his own, which was to make sane people crazy."

"That was turning the tables with a vengeance," drawled "Dye," from his perch on an upturned pail. "I wonder if he was any relation to 'Cutlets'?"

"A lineal ancestor, I'll bet a biscuit," chimed in "Hay." "Don't you remember the quotation, 'By these acts you will know their forefathers,' or something like that?"

"Well," resumed "Stump," "the crazy captain put the doctor and the crew in the cages and began to feed them hardtack and berth-deck scouse and salt-horse and——"

THE SEARCHLIGHT "SWEEPING BACK AND FORTH ACROSS THE BLACK OF THE HORIZON" (*page* 175).

"Must have been a Government naval contractor in his time," murmured "Morrie."

"I bet I know the rest," exclaimed the "Kid," coming up in time to grasp the situation. "The captain set his prisoners to carrying coal from the after hold forward and then back again, didn't he?"

"If you fellows think you can tell the story better than I can, go ahead," retorted "Stump," in disgust. "You are like a lot of old maids at a sewing circle. I give——"

"What was that?" suddenly cried "Hay," springing to his feet. "If it wasn't a flash of light I'll eat my——"

A figure hastily emerged from the gloom aft.

"Go to your stations at once, you men," called out a voice. "General quarters!"

As we scurried toward the hatch a great shaft of light appeared off the port beam, and began sweeping back and forth across the black of the horizon.

"Good heavens!" exclaimed "Hay," "it's a searchlight on some man-of-war. We're in for it now!"

CHAPTER XIII.

A NARROW ESCAPE.

The finger of light sweeping the heavens above the distant horizon meant to us the presence either of friend or foe, and the question was one we had little desire to solve at that moment. Rumors of Spanish warships lurking in the waters adjacent to Cuba were rife, and it had even been stated that another squadron inferior only to Cervera's fleet was somewhere in the neighborhood.

We of the "Yankee" were willing, and I may say, without undue boasting, eager to meet any vessel of equal size or even larger, but to give battle to a whole fleet was a little too much. Nevertheless, when the word was passed to go to "general quarters," there was no sulking nor hesitancy.

The battery was ready in record time.

Our gun was placed in trim, ammunition hatches opened, cartridges whipped on deck, and the piece prepared for instant use so rapidly that the officer of the division, Lieutenant Greene, gave us warm praise.

Then we waited.

It is difficult for a layman—a citizen who has not experienced the test of action and danger in battle—to understand or appreciate our feelings that night. It is hard to describe them, to paint with mere words the intense seriousness and gravity of the situation. You can imagine a dark night at sea—a night so black that the senses feel oppressed. You can add to these a thrill of impending danger and a vision of capture by a cruel enemy and the thought that the very next second will sound the signal for an uproar and outbreak of combat, but your impressions will fall far short of the reality—that must be experienced to be appreciated.

As we stood at our stations surrounding Number Eight gun, I tried to read the faces of my companions, to see if I could find in them traces of worry or anxiety, or of fear. The situation warranted even the latter emotion. The dim light cast by the flickering battle lanterns sent fantastic shadows dancing over deck and bulkhead, and caused the men at the guns to resemble, in their stained white working clothes, so many gaunt spectres.

But they were spectres with a grim purpose in view, and as the officer of the division strode back and forth, alert and watchful, they followed his movements with their eyes, eager for the word that would set them in action. They were not veterans, and their experience in war could have been measured by days, but they were honestly ready to fight and to shed the last drop of their blood for the flag waving over the taffrail.

It was a ticklish situation. Even the "Kid," with his careless, happy-go-lucky mind, would have admitted that; but as time passed without bringing a break in the monotony of waiting, we began to feel restless. The tension was still great, but the first sense of apprehension was gone.

"I do wish something would happen," muttered "Hay," after a while. "Can you see anything from that port, 'Morrie'?"

"A wall of blackness, that's all," replied the Rochester man.

"We've changed our course several times," spoke up Flagg. "I think the 'old man' is scooting for cover."

"Fool if he didn't," growled Tommy. "They have a pretty habit of court-martialling naval officers when they risk their ship unnecessarily.

If Captain Brownson should fail to do all in his power to escape from what his judgment tells him is overwhelming odds, he'd find himself in trouble. Discretion is the better part of valor, even in the navy."

Suddenly we began to notice a peculiar glow tinging the darkness, and reflecting from the polished parts of the gun. It came suddenly and with a spurt of ruddy light unmistakable.

"It's a fire somewhere," exclaimed Flagg. "Look! it's getting brighter."

"It comes from this ship," cried "Stump," edging toward the port. "Is it possible the old hooker is on fire?"

We waited for the ringing of the alarm bell, or the call to "fire quarters," but the minutes slipped by without the summons. Outside, the ruddy glare tinged the surface of the sea, sparkling from foam-crested waves, and forming a circle of dancing light through which the "Yankee" speeded on in her flight for safety.

Our curiosity increased apace, and we watched eagerly for passing messengers or for some stray word that would explain the peculiar phenomenon. It was Kennedy who finally solved the mystery—Kennedy the luckless, he whom we dubbed "Lucky Bag," because of his propensity to allow his wearing apparel to find its way into the clutches of "Jimmy Legs." Kennedy had slipped near the port and was trying to perform the difficult feat of scanning the upper deck from the opening.

"Come back here and stop that 'rubbernecking,' No. 7," called out Tommy. "Do you want to get on the report?"

"For the hundred and 'steenth time," added "Stump," with a grin.

"Perhaps he's seasick," suggested "Dye."

"It's about due. He hasn't heaved up his boots since noon."

"Did you hear what 'Cutlets' said to him yesterday?" spoke up "Hay." "He was 'wigging' Kennedy, and he remarked in his tender way, 'Look here, you hero, why don't you brace up and be a man? You are continually sick or on the report, and you aren't worth your salt. Get down below now, and fill your billet.' Poor devil! he tries to do his best, I guess."

Just then Kennedy faced around toward us and we saw that he was laughing.

"What do you think?" he said. "It's a fire after all."

"A fire? Where?" we gasped simultaneously.

"In the furnaces. I saw a big flame leaping from the funnel. Gee! they must be whooping

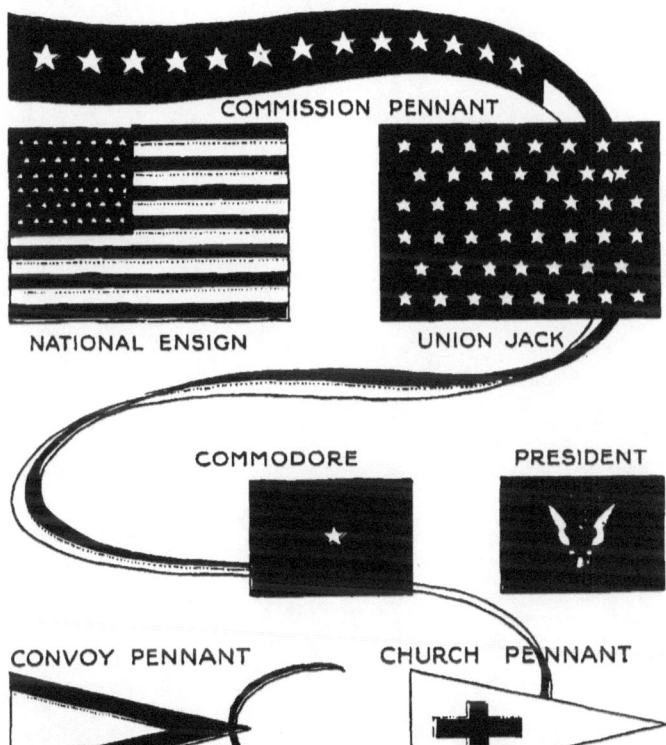

her up below to beat the band. Coal piled up to the top of the flues."

"It's oil," exclaimed Tommy, gravely. "They are feeding the fires with crude oil. That means the last resort, fellows. The 'old man' is trying to get every ounce of steam possible."

Our curiosity satisfied, we felt more at ease, and we lounged at our stations and listened to the banging of furnace doors and grating of shovels in the fire room below. Occasionally one of us would venture an opinion or try to exchange views, and "Stump" even started a story, but in the main we were quiet and watchful.

From the swaying and trembling of the hull it was evident the "Yankee" was being pushed at her utmost speed. Mess gear rattled in the chests, the deck quivered, and from down in the lower depths came the quick throb-throb of the overworked engines. Presently the red glare caused by the upleaping flames from the funnel died away, and darkness settled down again.

"I guess we are making it," observed Tommy. "We have been a good two hours racing at this gait, which means a matter of almost forty miles."

"They might let us take a run on deck,"

grumbled Flagg. "What's the use of holding up this gun all night? It's getting monotonous."

"Here comes the 'Kid,'" exclaimed "Dye."
"He may have some news."

The youngster brought a message to Lieutenant Greene. As he started off, he whispered:

"We are going to 'secure' in a few moments. It has been a great scoot. I heard the captain say to 'Mother Hubbub' that it would go down in history as a masterly retreat."

"Was it a Spanish fleet?" queried "Hay."

"They are not certain. The skipper now thinks that it was a convoy of transports bringing the army of occupation. He didn't stop to find out, though. Say, you fellows look tired. Why don't you 'pipe down'?"

He scurried off with a laugh, and we were just settling back for another siege of it when the welcome order came to "secure." The order was executed in a jiffy, and then those who had the off watch piled into their hammocks with a celerity seldom equalled. Santiago was reached early the following morning, and before the day was over we heard that our neighbors of the night before were, as the captain had suspected, a fleet of transports bringing troops from the United States.

A NARROW ESCAPE.

"Which doesn't alter the fact that we displayed wisdom in taking a 'sneak,'" commented Tommy, grimly. "It's a clever chief who knows when to retreat."

The great gray ships still tossed idly on the rolling blue sea when we took our station at the right of the line.

It seemed more like a panorama, arranged for the amusement of an admiring crowd, than a fleet of floating forts ready at a moment's notice to pour out death and destruction.

The flagship "New York," gay with signal bunting, was the centre of a fleet of launches and small boats. The boats' crews, in white duck, lounged in their places, while the captains were aboard conferring with the admiral.

The torpedo boat "Porter" flashed in and out between the grim battleships in an almost playful way.

A signal boy on the "Brooklyn" held a long wigwag conversation with the flagship, the bit of bright color showing sharply against the lead-colored turret.

It was hard to realize that only a few days ago these same ships, that now rested so calmly and majestically, were enveloped in clouds of smoke, their great guns spitting forth fire and a fearful hail of steel.

We looked at picturesque old Morro on the bluff, and there, close to the lighthouse, still floated the Spanish colors. It was aggravating, and we would like to have shot the hateful bunting away.

We had no sooner reached our station than the boatswain's call echoed from one end of the ship to the other, "Away gig." Whereupon the gig's crew rushed below and "broke out" clean whites. No matter what happens, the gig's crew must always be clean, both in person and apparel.

Our gig soon joined the fleet of waiting boats at the flagship's gangway, and lay there while the captain went aboard.

The skipper returned about noon and went forward. Immediately, we heard the cry "All hands on the gig falls." Then, before the boat was fairly out of water, we heard the engine bell jingle.

We were off again.

Some active member of the "Rumor Committee" said we were bound for Jamaica. And after consultation with a signal boy, who came aft to read the patent log, we found that we were heading for that island.

The wind was dead ahead and blowing fresh and cool, but the sun was hot, and the boat-

"EVERY HOUR A SIGNAL BOY CAME RUNNING AFT TO READ THE LOG" (*page* 185).

"ALL HANDS ON THE CAT FALLS!" (*page* 186).

swain's mates were instructed to keep the men in the shade as much as possible.

The stress and strain of the night before made the few hours of "caulking off," that we now enjoyed, particularly grateful.

We lay so thick on the windward side of the spar deck under the awning, that it would have been difficult to find foot room.

Every hour a signal boy came running aft to read the log, which was attached to the taffrail on the starboard quarter. The log worked on the same principal as a bicycle cyclometer. It had two dials that indicated the miles and fractions of miles as they were reeled off. A long, braided line, having what we called a "twister" attached, trailed behind in the water and made the wheels go round, a certain number of revolutions to the mile.

Hour after hour the ship rushed through the water. The engines throbbed in a regular, settled sort of way, that reminded one of a man snoring. The wind blew softly and caressingly. The ship rolled easily in the long swell. It was soothing and restful, and we felt quite reconciled to life in the navy. We almost forgot that we were on an engine of war; that there was enough ammunition below to blow up several "Maine's," and that we were cruising in the enemy's country.

The men talked cheerfully of home, pursuits, and pleasures, for it was too fine, too bright, to be depressed.

Finally the sun went down in a blaze of glory, dropping suddenly into the sea as it is wont to do in the tropics.

In a few minutes it was dark. In these latitudes there is practically no twilight; the sun jumps into his full strength in the morning, and quenches his glory in the sea before one realizes the day is gone.

Soon after dark the lookouts began to report lights, and before long we found ourselves steaming into a fine harbor, which we learned was Port Antonio.

A delightful feeling of security stole over us. We were at anchor in a friendly port, the inhabitants of which spoke the same tongue as we did and sympathized with us. We turned in at the earliest possible moment, and as we lay in our " elevated folding beds," as " Hay " called them, we could hear unmistakable shore sounds —the barking of dogs, the crowing of cocks, and according to some active imaginations, even the bell of a trolley car.

At one o'clock we were wakened by the call, " All hands on the cat falls." We slipped out of our " dream bags " with the best grace we could muster, and went forward to pull up the anchor to its place on the forecastle deck.

So we gave up the pleasant idea that we were to spend the night undisturbed, and the guns' crews of the watch on deck made themselves as comfortable as possible under the circumstances, on their wooden couch around the guns; viz., the deck.

When the sun rose next morning, we found that land was plainly visible from the port side, and we soon learned that we were still in Jamaican waters and would arrive at Montego Bay about ten o'clock.

The programme was carried out to the dot.

The "Yankee" steamed into the beautiful bay, the crew "at quarters," in honor of the English man-of-war "Indefatigable," which lay at anchor there, and we had hardly let down our anchor when a fleet of "bumboats" came chasing out to us.

Though an American warship had never visited this port before, we seemed to be recognized by these enterprising marine storekeepers as easy prey.

The native "bumboat" is a dugout affair very narrow for its length, and seemingly so cranky that we marvelled at the size of the sail carried. They brought fruits of all kinds, and tobacco, so we didn't stop to criticise their rig, but showed plainly that we were right glad to see them.

The boatmen and women were all colored people and, like the race the world over, were most fantastically and gaily clothed. The women wore bright-hued calico dresses, and brighter bandana handkerchiefs on their heads. The men wore flaming neckties, gay shirts, and, in some cases, tall white or gray beaver hats.

The boats were filled with yellow, green, and red fruits and brightly-colored packages of tobacco, the whole making a most vivid and brilliant display of color.

The crew bought eagerly, regardless of price. Limes, oranges, mangoes, bananas, and pineapples came over the side in a steady stream, while an equally steady, though smaller, stream of silver went back to the boats.

It was a harvest day for the Montego Bay "bumboatmen."

Though we bought the fruits without hesitation, we bit into them gingerly, for, to most of us, many of them were strange.

Tom LeValley brought me a mango and said that I could have it if I would sample it and tell what it was like. I accepted, for I had not been

A NARROW ESCAPE.

lucky enough to get near a boat to buy for myself.

He handed me something that looked like a pear but was of the color of an orange. I was just about to bite into it when I chanced to look up. I saw that I was the target of all eyes. Putting on a bold front, I sunk my teeth in the yellow rind. I found it was pleasant to the taste, but unlike anything that I had ever put in my mouth before. Still the fellows gazed at me. Was it a trick mango I had tackled so recklessly? I determined not to be stumped, and took a good big bite. In a moment, I discovered why I was the "observed of all observers." The last bite loosened a good deal of the peel, and the thing began to ooze. It oozed through my fingers and began to run down my sleeve; it dripped on my trousers and made an ineradicable stain; my face was smeared with it, my hands were sticky with it, my mouth was full of it, and still the blamed thing oozed.

Then the unfeeling crowd laughed. Some one shouted "get under the hose." Another yelled "Swab ho," whereupon a none too clean deck swab was brought and applied to my face and hands, protests being unavailing.

I afterwards remarked to Tom that he had better try experiments on himself, or present me with a bathtub along with the next mango, and I have since learned that a Distinguished Person came to the same conclusion when first introduced to this deceitful fruit.

We enjoyed our stay in this beautiful island port very much, and it was with great reluctance that we obeyed the order to "haul on the cat falls." As we were walking away with that heavy line, we saw a liberty party from the English warship start for shore in the ship's cutters, and we envied them with all our hearts.

The town looked very attractive, set as it was on the side and at the base of a high hill, the red-tiled roofs of its houses showing against the graceful, green palm trees. On our left, a grove of cocoanut palms flourished, and beneath grazed a herd of cattle.

Soon the ship began to back out, and then, as the bay grew wider, she turned slowly and headed for the open.

"Lash your mess chests," said messenger "Kid" to the berth deck cooks. "Orders from the officer of the deck," he added.

He turned to us, who were standing by the open port. "I guess we'll have a lively time of it, for I heard 'Cutlets' say the barometer is dropping at a terrible rate."

The "Kid" scurried further aft to give the

order to the boatswain's mates and master-at-arms.

We looked out to seaward and noted the black sky and the rising wind.

"I guess you 'heroes' will have a chance to show what right you have to be called seamen," said "Stump," mimicking "Cutlets."

CHAPTER XIV.

WE ENGAGE IN A SEA FIGHT.

"Watch on deck, put on your oilers," shouted the boatswain's mates.

The order came none too soon, for as the last man ran up the companion-way ladder, the rain began to drop in sheets.

The rising wind drove the rain in our faces with stinging force, and we were soon wet as drowned rats.

The white-capped seas raced alongside, and the "Yankee" heaved and tossed like a bucking bronco. The lookouts at the masthead swayed forward and back, to and fro, dizzily, and the officer of the deck on the bridge had difficulty in keeping his feet. The pots and pans in the galley banged noisily, and ever and anon the screw was lifted out of the water, and for a few turns shook the ship from stern to stem with its accelerated speed.

A number of men who had partaken too freely of tropical fruits manned the rail and seemed too much interested in the seething water below to notice the rain that was dripping down their necks.

For a time, things were very lively aboard the old hooker, and, though in the main unpleasant, the grandeur of the sea in the tempest made up for all discomforts. The flash of the lightning, the roar of the thunder, the hum and whistle of the wind through the rigging, and the swish of the seas as they dashed themselves to spray against the sides of the ship—all this made an impressive chorus, more stirring even than the roar of cannon and the shriek of shell.

When "hammocks" was blown by the ship's bugler at a quarter to seven, we found it difficult to make our way forward to the nettings. One moment we were toiling up the deck's steep incline; the next, the ship would bury her prow, and we were rushing forward pell mell. The boat seemed to be endowed with diabolical intelligence that night. A man might, perchance, stoop to tie his shoe or examine a freshly stubbed toe, when the ship would seem to divine that she had him at a disadvantage, and would leap forward so that he would immediately stand on his head, or affectionately and firmly embrace a convenient stanchion. "Pride cometh before a fall," and the man who thought he had caught the swing and could walk a chalk line on the deck, soon found that the old boat knew a new trick or two, and in a twinkling of an eye he was sawing the air frantically with his arms, in his efforts to keep his balance.

Though the force of the tropical storm was soon spent, the sea continued high, and locomotion was difficult.

The hammocks were given out by the "hammock stowers" of the watch on duty. They called out the numbers stenciled on our "dream bags," and the owners stepped forward and claimed them. As soon as a man secured his hammock he immediately slung it in place, unlashed it, and arranged the blankets to his liking.

A group gathered around the capstan aft, after the hammock ceremony had been completed.

Some one said, "I'm glad I can sleep in a hammock a night like this; the heave of the ship will be hardly felt."

"Yes," responded the "Kid," "I wouldn't swap my 'sleeping bag' for the captain's bed, to-night."

"That reminds me," said "Stump." "Speaking of beds—when we were in New York a friend of mine came aboard to see me. He had a sister, but left her at home."

"You can thank your lucky stars he did. If she'd seen your weary, coal-covered visage, you could not even have been a brother to her," interrupted "Hay."

"I guess you're right," responded "Stump," with an appreciative grin. "Anyhow, she did not come. So when her brother got home she plied him with questions—this he wrote me afterwards—wanted to know how I looked, asked what the ship was like, inquired about our food, and then she questioned him about my stateroom. Was it prettily decorated? Whose photograph occupied the place of honor on my dressing table?

"Billy, my friend," explained "Stump," "is a facetious sort of chap, so he told her that of course such a large crew could not *all* have staterooms, but *I* had a very nice one, that could be folded when not in use, and put to one side out of the way. It was made of canvas, he said, so constructed that it would always swing with the ship, and so keep upright in a rolling sea.

"She listened intently, and finally broke out enthusiastically: 'How nice!'

"Billy almost had a fit at that, and I nearly had, when I read his letter."

We all laughed heartily and trooped below to

enjoy a few hours' sleep in our "folding staterooms."

The next day dawned bright and clear, and warm; with nothing to remind us of the storm of the night before except the seedy look on the faces of some of the "heroes" who were prone to seasickness.

The sun had not been up many hours when the masthead lookout shouted, "Sail ho!" To which the officer of the deck replied, "Where away?"

"Dead ahead, sir. Looks like one of the vessels of the fleet, sir."

And so we joined the squadron again, after an absence of twenty-four hours.

Nothing had occurred while we were away. Cervera's fleet was still "bottled up" in Santiago harbor, and the American fleet held the cork so effectively that even a torpedo boat could not get out.

After preparing the ship for the usual Sunday inspection, and arraying ourselves in clean whites, polished shoes, and stockings, we thought we had done all the work that would be required of us for the day. But when the gig returned, bringing the skipper from the flagship, we learned that we were to get under way right after dinner, and steam to the westward.

WE ENGAGE IN A SEA FIGHT.

After " turn to " was sounded at 1:15 o'clock, we noted a long string of signal flags flying from the signal yard, which we found requested permission from the flagship to proceed at once. As the affirmative pennant on the " New York " slowly rose to its place on the foremast, the " Yankee's " jingle bell sounded, and the ship began to gather headway.

At " afternoon quarters "—1:30—a drill, new to us, was taught; called by the officers " physical drill," and by the men " rubber-necking." We hardly felt the need of exercise. The swinging of a swab and use of sand and canvas, to say nothing of " scrub and wash clothes" before breakfast, seemed to us sufficient work to keep our muscles in good condition; but it is one of the axioms in the navy that " Satan finds some mischief still for idle hands to do," so the men were soon lined up—sufficient space being given each man to allow him to swing his arms, windmill fashion, without interfering with his neighbor.

A regular calisthenic exercise was gone through, such as may be seen in gymnasiums all over the country; but instead of a steady, even floor, upon which it would be quite easy to stand tiptoe, on one foot, or crouched with bended knees, it was quite a different matter to do these "stunts" on the constantly rolling deck.

At the order, "Knee stoop, one," we bent our knees till we sat on our heels. "Heads up, hands on the hips, there!" said Mr. Greene of our division, as some one obeyed an almost irresistible impulse to keep his balance by putting out his hand. The man obeyed, but at that instant the ship gave a lurch, and the poor chap fell over on his head and almost rolled down the berth-deck hatch.

The laugh that followed was promptly suppressed, and though the exercise was not carried out with a great deal of grace or ease, Mr. Greene seemed to be satisfied with the first attempt.

We steamed along all the afternoon past the coast of Cuba and within plain sight of the beautiful, surf-rimmed beach. We looked for signs of the enemy, but not a living thing could be seen. Not a sign of human habitation; not an indication that any human being had ever set foot on this desolate land. So beautiful, so grand, so lonely was it that we longed to go ashore and shout, just to set a few echoes reverberating in the hills.

Toward night, we turned seaward, and the land was lost to view; at the same time the

WE ENGAGE IN A SEA FIGHT.

"Yosemite," manned by the Michigan Naval Reserves, who had accompanied us thus far, dropped out of sight in the haze. She was bound for Jamaica.

A ship painted the "war color" now in vogue in the United States navy, will disappear as if by magic when dusk comes on. The lead color makes any object covered with it invisible in half light or a haze.

There had been much speculation during the day and evening as to our probable destination, but we remained in ignorance until the next morning, when it became known that our orders were to call at the port of Cienfuegos, a prominent city of southern Cuba, some three hundred and thirty miles from Santiago.

It was reported that the object of our visit was to intercept and capture a blockade runner said to be aiming for that port. The news received an enthusiastic welcome fore and aft. The billet of "fleet messenger" was becoming tiresome.

The land had been sighted at two bells (nine o'clock), and all hands were looking for Cienfuegos, but it was past one before the mouth of the harbor was gained. The "Yankee's" crew were at regular quarters at the time, but a hurried order to dismiss and clear ship for action sent the different guns' crews scurrying to their stations.

To add to the interest, word came from the bridge to train the guns aft and to do everything possible to disguise the cruiser.

"We are to masquerade as a blooming merchantman," chuckled "Dye." "This reminds me of my boyhood days when I read pirate stories. Do you remember that yarn about Kydd, where he rigged painted canvas about his ship and hid all the ports, 'Stump'? It was great. The whole piratical crew, with the exception of a dozen men, kept below, and when a poor unfortunate ship came along, the bloodthirsty villains captured her."

"I wish they had caught you at the same time," retorted "Stump." "Then we wouldn't be bothered with your infernal cackle. Here, give me a hand with this mess chest."

By this time the task of preparing for action was an old story, and we made short work of it. The call to "general quarters" followed without delay, and, as we prepared the battery for action, word came from above that a large gunboat, showing Spanish colors, was leaving the harbor in our direction.

"Which means a scrap of the liveliest description," muttered Tommy. "They evidently take

WE ENGAGE IN A SEA FIGHT.

us for a trader without guns, and they'll attack us sure."

Boom!

A six-pounder gave voice from the spar deck, instantly followed by a five-inch breechloader in the waist. Number Eight was loaded, and "Hay," who held the firing lanyard, snatched another sight, then stood erect with left hand in the air.

"Ready, sir," he called out to the officer of the division.

"Fire!" came the reply promptly.

With the word a vicious report shook the deck, and the gun muzzle vanished in a cloud of smoke. Eager hands opened the breech, others inserted another cartridge, there was a shifting of the training lever, a turn of the elevating wheel, then "Hay" stood back once more, and coolly made the electrical connection.

Following the second report came a dull, booming sound, apparently from a distance. We eyed one another significantly.

"It's a fort," quoth "Dye." "We've got to tackle both sea and land forces."

Presently, while we were hard at work sending shots at the Spanish gunboat, which was in lively action a short distance away, we became aware of a peculiar whirring noise—a sound like the angry humming of a swarm of hornets. It would rise and fall in volume, then break off short with a sharp crash. Suddenly, while glancing through the port, I saw something strike the surface, sending up a great spurt of water. It was followed by a dull, muffled report which seemed to shake the ship.

It was a shell!

"Whiz! they are coming pretty fast," remarked Flagg. "That last one didn't miss us by a dozen yards."

"This isn't Santiago shooting," put in Tommy. "These beggars know how to aim."

During the next ten minutes the fighting was fast and furious. It was load and fire and load again without cessation. There was the old trouble in regard to the smoke, and half the time we had to aim blindly. Notwithstanding that fact, "Hay" did so well that word came from Captain Brownson complimenting him warmly.

The "Yankee" seemed to be the centre of a series of eruptions. The Spanish shells kept the water continually boiling, and with the splashing of each projectile there would arise a geyser-like fountain accompanied by a muffled explosion which could be plainly felt on board the ship.

"THERE WAS TEMPORARY CONFUSION" (*page* 203).

WE ENGAGE IN A SEA FIGHT.

It was the first real naval battle experienced by us—the bombardment of Santiago being of an entirely different calibre—and it needed only the grewsome setting of surgeons and wounded and blood to make it complete. That soon came.

We of Number Eight gun were working at our stations, so intent on our duties that the uproar of shot and shell outside claimed little attention, when suddenly there came a louder explosion than usual directly in front of the open port.

There was a blinding flash, a puff of stifling smoke, and then Kennedy, who was just approaching the gun with a shell, staggered back, and almost fell to the deck. Tommy, the first captain, made a gesture as if brushing something from his breast, and then leaped to the injured man's assistance.

"It was a piece of shell," cried "Stump." "It came through the port."

There was temporary confusion. The surgeon and his assistants came on a run, but before they could reach the spot, Kennedy recovered and advanced to meet them. He presented a horrible spectacle, with his face and neck and body spattered with blood, and we who were nearest saw that he had been frightfully wounded in the left shoulder.

Notwithstanding that fact, he remained cool and steady, and never made the slightest indication that he was suffering. When he finally disappeared down the berth-deck ladder we exchanged glances of surprise and sympathy.

"That isn't Kennedy," murmured "Stump," softly.

"We didn't know him after all," said "Hay." "Poor devil! I hope he isn't badly injured."

"He has been in the hardest kind of luck since we left New York," spoke up Tommy. "Seasick half the time, always in trouble, and bucking against homesickness and everything else. And now he has to be wounded. It's a shame."

Our thoughts were with our comrade as we served the gun, and when word came a few moments later that he was doing fairly well, we could hardly repress a cheer.

There was little time, however, for displaying emotion. We were right in the thick of the fight, and the "Yankee's" battery was being worked to the limit. It seemed as if the air fairly reeled with the noise and clamor of combat. Shells buzzed and shrieked about us, and smoke gathered in thick, stifling clouds all about the ship.

While we were laboring, stripped to the waist,

WE ENGAGE IN A SEA FIGHT.

and trying our utmost to disable or sink the Spanish gunboat, an incident was occurring on deck which seemed more fitted for the pages of a novel than those of a story of facts.

It was a display of daredevil courage seldom equalled in warfare.

The lad whom we familiarly termed the "Kid" was the central figure and the hero. The diary of No. 5 of the after port gun, from which this narrative is taken, says of him: "'Kid' Thompson is the ship's human mascot and all-round favorite with officers and men. His bump of respect is a depression, but his fund of ready wit and his unvarying good nature are irresistible. He is eighteen years of age, and is a 'powder monkey' on Number Sixteen, a six-pounder on the spar deck. This gun and Number Fifteen were the last to obey the order to cease firing during the bombardment of Santiago."

During the fight with the Spanish gunboat it chanced that the port battery was not engaged for a brief period, so the "Kid," with the rest of Number Sixteen crew, were at rest. To better see the shooting the "Kid" climbed upon the after wheel-house roof. The shells from the gunboat and the forts were dropping all around, fore and aft, port and starboard; they whistled through the rigging, and exploded in every direction, sending their fragments in a veritable hail of metal on all sides.

The fact that the "Yankee" had so far escaped injury aroused in the "Kid's" breast a feeling of the utmost contempt for the Spanish gunners. Coolly standing upon his feet, he assumed the pose of a baseball player, and holding a capstan bar in his hands, called out tauntingly:

"Here, you dagoes, give me a low ball, will you? Put 'em over the plate!"

As a shell would fly past with a shriek, he would strike at it, shouting at the same time:

"Put 'em over the plate, I say. Do you expect me to walk up to the fo'c's'le to get a rap at 'em? Hi, there! wake up!"

Then as a shot fell short, he laughed: "Look at that drop, will you? Do you think I'm going to dive for it?"

A moment later a shell flew past so close that the windage almost staggered him, but the daring lad only cried banteringly: "That's more like it. One more a little closer and I'll show you a home run worth seeing."

And so it went until he was espied from the bridge and peremptorily ordered down.

In the meantime, while this little episode was in progress, we on the gun deck were laboring

WE ENGAGE IN A SEA FIGHT.

without cessation. A dozen shots had been fired from Number Eight alone, when suddenly another fort secured the range, and began a deadly fusillade.

The situation was becoming extremely serious!

CHAPTER XV.

COALING IN THE TROPICS.

The well-directed fire of the forts at the entrance to Cienfuegos was rapidly making the "Yankee's" position untenable, and it soon became apparent that we would have to give way before overwhelming odds. Fifteen minutes after the battle began between the Spanish gunboat and the "Yankee," the former beat a hasty retreat, steaming back into the harbor.

It was plainly evident, however, that she had been badly hulled, as she yawed wildly while passing from sight behind the headlands. This of itself was victory enough for the present, and at the end of twenty minutes' firing, we withdrew out of range.

Our object in the first place was, as we ascertained from forward during the day, to intercept a Spanish blockade runner, the "Purissima Concepcion"; so we laid off the harbor and waited for the coming of the ship, which was supposed to have left Jamaica for Cienfuegos. The day was spent in cleaning up after our brief but lively battle, and when night came, we were again shipshape.

Shortly after daybreak the following morning, the lookout aloft reported that a steamer, evidently a man-of-war, was emerging from the harbor. The crew were called to "general quarters" at once, and every preparation made to give the stranger a lively reception. She proved, however, to be the German warship "Geier" bound for Santiago.

"In time of peace prepare for war" is a good adage, but the reverse is also true. Peaceful pursuits are of a necessity carried out even in the face of the enemy.

At "evening quarters" new hammocks were doled out, and all hands were instructed to scrub the old ones next morning and turn them in.

By this time we had become quite expert laundrymen, but we had never tackled a stiff canvas hammock, and the prospect was far from pleasant; the following morning, however, we learned how to perform this final feat of cleansing; after which we felt qualified to wash anything—from a handkerchief to a circus tent.

As "Hay" said, "I feel equal to applying for the position of general housework man, if I lose my job. I can sew—you ought to see the elegant patch I put on the seat of my old blues—I can 'scrub and wash' clothes, I can sweep beautifully, I can make a bed with neatness and despatch. And I have been known to get on my knees and scrub the deck."

"You're not the only one," growled Bill. "Why, even 'Dirty Greene' escapes the aforetime customary 'calling down.'"

Greene was a clever fellow, a student at Harvard, the owner of a yacht, and a good sailor, but his college education did not help him to get his clothes clean. That was a study that had been left out of his university curriculum. The consequence was that he, with a good many others, was "called down" at every inspection.

"Greene is getting it in the neck now," said his friend "Steve"; "but I think he will get even some day with his cousin, the lieutenant of his division."

"How's that?" we chorused.

"Why, you see he owns a schooner yacht. And his cousin, the lieutenant, is very fond of sailing and never fails to accept an invitation to go cruising on her. Some day when the lieutenant is aboard, Greene will look him over and discover that his shoes are not polished, that his hair has not been combed properly, or his white duck trousers are not immaculate. He will then be sent below in disgrace to repair these faults, and our friend Greene will have the merry Ha! Ha! on him. 'He who laughs last, laughs best.'"

We one and all wished we owned yachts and could invite some of the other officers—" Cutlets " in particular.

Blockading duty is monotonous work, though the strain on the lookouts is intense. During the day, a bright lookout must be kept for the lightest tinge of smoke on the horizon, and at night for the faintest glimmer of light, or a deeper shadow on the rim of the ocean that would betray a ship.

It was Tuesday night, and time hung heavy on our hands. Eight bells had not sounded, and, though hammocks had been given out, neither watch could turn in. It was with particular glee, therefore, that we welcomed the news that " Steve " had composed an up-to-date verse to his " Tommy Atkins " song. After some persuasion—for he is a modest chap—he consented to sing it for us.

> " The first two verses of this song were writ
> Before we sailed away for Cuba's Isle;
> And since that time the Spaniards we have fit,
> And chased their gunboats many a weary mile.

A GUNNER ABOARD THE "YANKEE."

We've heard the bullets whistling overhead,
　We've heard the shells fly by and called it sport,
　　And down at Cienfuegos
　　We proved ourselves courageous
　By tackling both a gunboat and a fort.

CHORUS.

　"Now we'd *like* to run a ferry,
　　All along the Jersey shore ;
　　Fighting Spaniards, it is very
　　　Nice, but we don't want—no more.
　　We would give our bottom dollar,
　　　And of that you need not fear,
　　Just to hear the masthead holler
　　　Brooklyn navy yard is here."

"That's very good, 'Steve,'" said Greene, "but I can't quite agree to that line: 'Fighting Spaniards it is very nice, but we don't want—no more.' I'd like to have a few more raps at 'em."

"You are such a bloodthirsty chap," said Flagg, "you slam the charges into your old Number Seven as if you would like to wipe out the whole enemy with one fell swoop."

"Well," replied Greene, thoughtfully, "a man does get awfully excited when the guns begin to bark."

And every one of us knew exactly how he felt.

COALING IN THE TROPICS.

We maintained a close vigil until the sixteenth of June—two days later—then sailed for Santiago. Shortly after entering port we were informed that the Spanish gunboat with which we had been engaged off Cienfuegos had sunk, sent to the bottom by our fire; a bit of news highly appreciated.

Our stay in Santiago was short, the "Yankee" leaving for Guantanamo the next day at eleven o'clock. On reaching the latter port we found evidences of a considerable change in the condition of affairs. On our former visit, as the reader will remember, we had engaged in an interesting argument with a gunboat, a blockhouse, and a fort, driving the boat back into the harbor and silencing the fort. The good work done that day had borne fruit.

On entering the bay we found several of our vessels quietly riding at anchor—the "Oregon," "Marblehead," "Dolphin" (of railway-train fame), the ambulance ship "Solace," the "Panther," "Suwanee," and three or four colliers and despatch boats.

But that which attracted our instant attenion and brought an involuntary cheer from us, was the sight of Old Glory, flaunting proudly from a tall flagstaff erected on the site of the former Spanish blockhouse.

"Hurray!" shouted "Stump," "it's the first American flag to fly over Cuba. And we dug the hole to plant it."

"That's right," assented "Dye." "We are the people."

"What's that camp on top of the hill?" queried Flagg, indicating a number of tents gleaming in dots of white against the background of green foliage.

"It is the marine camp," explained "Hay." "Didn't you hear about it in Santiago? Why, man, it's the talk of the fleet. The marine corps has been adding to its laurels again. The other day eight hundred of them landed from the "Panther" and fairly swept the place of Spaniards, fighting against three times their number. It was great."

"The marines have a fine record," put in Tommy. "I've been shipmates with them for years, and I am free to confess that they always do their duty."

"And are always faithful," remarked "Dye."

"That's their motto, 'Semper fidelis.' They have lived up to it in every war. They antedate the navy, you know."

"How's that?" asked the "Kid," who was willing to absorb knowledge at times.

Tommy produced an ancient book from his

ditty box, and proceeded to read an extract in a loud, sonorous voice. It was as follows:

"Resolved, That two battalions of marines be raised, consisting of one colonel, two lieutenant-colonels, two majors, and other officers, as usual in other regiments; that they consist of an equal number of privates with other battalions; that particular care be taken that no persons be appointed to offices or enlisted into said battalions but such as are good seamen, or so acquainted with maritime affairs as to be able to serve to advantage on sea when required, that they be enlisted and commissioned to serve for and during the present war with Great Britain and the colonies, unless dismissed by order of Congress, that they be distinguished by the names of the First and Second Battalions of Marines."

"The date of that resolution," added Tommy, with the air of a schoolmaster impressing a particular point, "is November 10, 1775, which was before any naval vessel had been sent to sea by the Continental Congress. So you see the marines can claim priority in point of service."

"And priority in point of landing in Cuba," added "Hod." "Here's to them."

Our discussion on the subject of marines was cut short by a summons to coal ship, a task which had come to form the greatest thorn in the flesh of all on board the "Yankee." The ship was run alongside the collier "Sterling," and the port watch was set to work at once.

From four to six and from eight to twelve p.m., and from four to eight the next morning the port watch shovelled, hoisted, and carried coal.

Coaling in the tropics is a very different thing from similar work in northern latitudes. The exertion of shovelling, or lifting the heavy baskets, added to the intense heat of the weather, makes of it a task extremely trying even to those of the strongest physique. During the time thus spent in Guantanamo two of the "Yankee's" crew were overcome by heat and exhaustion, and compelled to ask for medical attendance.

Our appearance beggared description. The exertion brought out a profuse perspiration on our half-naked bodies, to which the coal-dust stuck, thick and black. The black rubbed off in spots, showing the white skin beneath, the result being a most ludicrous mottled effect. A dime museum manager would make a fortune if he could have exhibited some of us as the piebald wild men from Guantanamo. It was not till afterward, however, that we could appreciate the humor of our looks. During the thick of the work we were too busy to note the funny

"OUR APPEARANCE BEGGARED DESCRIPTION" (page 216).

"TOOK ADVANTAGE OF THE TIME TO 'CAULK OFF'"
(page 220).

side of things; in fact, we felt quite sure that there was nothing funny about it. It is impossible to awaken the sense of humor in a man who is plying a heavy shovel in the hold of a collier, or lugging a weighty basket, while the temperature is soaring to unknown altitudes.

The ship had to be supplied with fuel, however, and as the crew had neglected to ingratiate themselves with a good-natured fairy to wish it aboard for them, they had to do the work with the best grace possible.

During a " spell " of resting, " Hay," who was a bit of a philosopher in his way, glanced about decks at the groups of panting, perspiring men, and remarked:

" It would be an object lesson to some of our friends in New York if they were to see us now. Just look at those fellows. Not one had ever before been compelled by ill-fortune to soil his hands with toil, yet when war threatened, and it was necessary to man ships in their country's service, they cheerfully took upon themselves the labors of a common sailor, and not only fought for the flag, but worked hard for it in menial tasks."

" Menial tasks is good," said " Dye," ruefully eyeing the baskets piled high with coal.

" Self-laudation is bad form," spoke up Flagg,

"but I think the Naval Reserves who are manning the different auxiliary cruisers—the "Yosemite," "Prairie," "Dixie," "Badger," "Yankee," and the monitors—as well as those serving on board the regular ships, should be given credit for their patriotism."

"The boys will get it when the time comes," remarked "Stump," confidently. "And while we are waiting we'll just carry a little more coal. Get in line there."

Kennedy, all this time, was bearing up under his trouble splendidly, and when the launch of the hospital ship "Solace" came alongside to take him away, we could hardly repress a cheer. He was lowered over the side in a chair. As the launch steamed away, carrying Kennedy and two other shipmates who had been overcome by heat, there was a lump in many a throat.

It was not until almost dark the next day that the bunkers were filled. At three bells (half-past five o'clock) we dropped the collier and steamed to sea en route down the coast. Shortly after ten the "Yankee" passed the fleet off Santiago. The electric searchlights in use on the ships nearer shore made a particularly brilliant display. The rays were turned directly upon the entrance to the harbor, and it was plainly evident that not even a small boat could emerge without being discovered.

All day Sunday we steamed out of sight of land, our course being to the westward and our speed a good fourteen knots.

For four hours in the morning we scrubbed the gun deck, washed the white paint work with fresh water and soap, scrubbed the deck with stiff "kiyi" brushes, and polished off the bright work. By noon the deck had its pristine immaculate look. We were in the midst of the sloppy job when "forecastle Murray" (one of the Murray twins—they looked so much alike that the invariable greeting in the morning was "How are you, Murray—or are you your brother?") came aft for a bucket of fresh water.

"What do you think of this?" he inquired pugnaciously. "Here we are scrubbing this blooming gun deck to beat the band, cleaning up the dirt of a two day's coaling, and now, forsooth, we are ploughing through the water at a fourteen or fifteen knot gait and burning up that coal almost as fast as we put it in."

He disappeared up the galley ladder, grumbling as he went.

"Another county heard from," said "Stump." "It does seem rather tough, but here goes"—he gave a vicious jerk to the hose he was handling and the stream caught "Hay" full in the neck, whereupon "Hay" saw to it that "Stump" had a salt-water bath.

By the time "mess gear" was piped, the ship was very clean, so during the afternoon we were left largely to our own devices. Some wrote letters, though the possibility of sending them or of receiving answers was very remote. Others gathered in little knots and read or sewed, and still others took advantage of the time to "caulk off" and make up some lost sleep.

And so passed another Sunday. Though we might not have a religious service we were certainly cleanly, and, therefore, at the worst, not far from godly.

Nothing of interest occurred until early Monday morning. Several minutes before "mess gear" was due, a lookout at the masthead reported smoke in sight off the starboard bow. The engine room was signalled for full steam, and the "Yankee" sped away in chase.

"It's our day for scrapping," said "Stump." "We've had more fighting on Monday than on any other day of the week. I wonder if it's a Spanish cruiser?"

"It is heading for Trinidad, whatever it is," remarked "Hay." "Do you see that sloping hill just ahead? It marks the entrance to the

"THE FUSILLADE WAS LIVELY" (*page* 221).

little port of Trinidad. If I am not mistaken we'll find a gunboat or two in the harbor."

"Hay" proved to be a prophet.

An hour later, on rounding a point of land, we came upon a small, armed launch steaming about near an old-time roofed-in gunboat which was riding at anchor in the harbor. As soon as we hove in sight the gunboat and launch opened fire. It was at long range, however, and the projectiles merely stirred up the water a mile away.

As the "Yankee's" guns replied, a two-masted steamer made her appearance from within the harbor and vanished behind the keys. The fusillade was lively, we firing fully one hundred rounds, but there was little damage done. After a time, the launch retreated, and we went outside for the night.

"It's the last of that scrap," remarked Tommy, the boatswain's mate, as he piped down. "We haven't any time to devote to such small fry."

CHAPTER XVI.

"REMEMBER THE FISH."

The following morning, after "all hands," the "Yankee" started westward along the coast. Cienfuegos was passed, and presently the cruiser was taken nearer shore. The lookouts were told to keep watch for horsemen riding near the beach. This order aroused our flagging interest, and the majority of men on board maintained a careful scrutiny of the white strip of land just beyond the breakers.

It was not until noon, however, that our search was rewarded. It was just after passing a deep inlet that one of the lookouts espied a group of men gathered near the water's edge. There seemed to be a number of them, and not far away could be seen a blue and white flag flying from a small staff.

The engines were stopped, and a boat officered by Lieutenant Duncan, and carrying "Hay" as interpreter, went ashore. "Hay" had spent several years in the West Indies and was thoroughly familiar with the Spanish language. As he was unique in that respect on board the ship, he often did duty as interpreter.

The boat landed in a little cove. After parleying for a while, one of the landing party was seen to wigwag. A few moments later the boat returned, bringing three Cubans, one of whom was the Cuban governor of Matanzas. The others were a captain and commander respectively. "Hay" was immediately surrounded and asked to describe what he saw ashore.

"I have had the honor of photographing a detachment of the Cuban Army of Liberation," he replied, quizzically. "To tell the truth, it looked like a part of Coxey's army. There were about thirty of them, and the clothing of the whole outfit wouldn't supply a New England farmer with a season's scarecrow. They carried guns of all descriptions, some of them with the barrels sawed off short like cavalry carbines; and not one of the men looked as if he knew the meaning of a square meal."

"Like Washington's army at Valley Forge, eh?" observed LeValley, joining the group.

"Yes, and they are fighting for their liberty, too."

"How did they like being photographed?" asked Tommy.

"Tickled to death. When I asked them to line up they almost fell over each other. Next to eating, I think the poor devils love to have their pictures taken. They were just like children, and when I pressed the button they stood round waiting for the photograph to drop from the kodak."

"Reminds me of the Cubans of Puerto Principe when the railway was built to that place," put in "Zere," the chief quartermaster. "A temporary roundhouse had been constructed, and when the first locomotive reached the city and was placed in it to be cleaned, all the natives from miles around gathered there. They crowded the windows and doors and were evidently waiting for something. Finally the engineer asked one of them what he wanted to see. 'We watch for mule to come out,' was the startling reply."

"Mule?" echoed Flagg.

"Yes, that was the only motive power known to them," grinned "Zere." "They thought even a Yankee engine must have a mule somewhere inside."

"That's like the natives of Guatemala," spoke up "Hop," the messenger. "When the street cars were introduced it was the usual thing for a native wishing to ride, to mount the platform and knock politely on the door. Some one inside would rise and open it, and then the native would enter and shake hands all round."

"Fancy doing that on a Broadway cable car," laughed "Stump."

Our imagination was not strong enough for that.

The Cuban guests remained with us for several hours, then went ashore, together with a boat-load of provisions contributed by the ship.

The whaleboat returned to the ship when the watch on deck had just been piped to supper. The other watch, therefore, had the job of pulling her up. The steady tramp, tramp, began and the boat slowly rose up foot by foot, till it was level with the rail, then there was a sudden jar and a crash. In an instant six men of the crew were in the water, while the boat floated away by itself.

There was a rush of feet on deck, loud shouts and cries of "Throw them a rope," "Set adrift the life buoy," "Where's that life belt?" and the like.

The men at mess jumped up, overturning cups and plates and dishes of food. One forecastle man pulled off his jumper and dove in to help.

The sea ladder was put over the side and

"Long Tommy" went down it, taking with him a piece of line; this he slipped under the arms of Rowland, the forecastle man, who had struck an oar on the way down, and was hurt. The man was soon hauled up on deck. The other four were also rescued. One went floating calmly off on the life buoy and was picked up by the gig, and the rest caught rope-ends and were safely hauled aboard, none the worse for their involuntary bath.

Lines were coiled down again, the sea ladder unshipped and put in its place, and soon all was quiet and shipshape again—but we discovered that two spit kits and a monkey-wrench had been thrown overboard to aid the sinking sailors.

"It's an ill wind that blows nobody good," quoted the "Kid," who happened to be sweeper that week. "I won't have to polish the brass on *those* kits again."

Shortly after the return of the last boat, smoke was sighted to seaward. The crew was called to general quarters without delay, and our ship steamed out to investigate. After a brief but exciting chase, we discovered that the supposed enemy was the auxiliary cruiser "Dixie," a sister ship of the "Yankee." She was manned by the Maryland Naval Reserves,

"REMEMBER THE FISH."

and her armament was composed of six-inch breechloading rifles, not of the rapid-fire class.

It soon became evident that her commanding officer, Commander Davis, was superior in rank to Commander Brownson, and he took charge of affairs at once. Captain Brownson was rowed over to the "Dixie" to pay his respects, and on his return a rumor that we were to be relieved of coast patrol duty by the "Dixie" and to proceed to Key West, went through the ship like wildfire.

Tom LeValley brought the news to a group of us gathered on the after gun deck. We were just discussing the peculiar, and apparently ridiculous, degrees of etiquette found among naval officers in general, as exemplified by the ranking of Commander Davis over Commander Brownson.

"They are both commanders," Tommy was explaining, "but Commander Davis happens to rank Commander Brownson by sixteen numbers in the official list. Both entered the service November 29, 1861, and——"

"Whoop!"

Down the ladder charged LeValley, wildly flourishing his cap. He stopped in front of us and gasped: "Hurrah! we're going—going to the United States, fellows."

" What's up? " demanded " Stump."

" The ' Dixie '——"

" Yes? "

" She's to relieve us, and we are ordered to Key West and then to New York. We're going——"

" Rats! " broke in " Hay," in disgust. " You can't give us any game like that. It's a rumor, my boy. We're never going home. The ' Yankee ' is the modern ' Flying Dutchman,' and——"

At that moment the "Kid" appeared in sight, and his beaming face convinced us. It was glorious news, but not one of us felt like cheering. Our emotions were too deep for that. The mere prospect of seeing home again was enough pleasure for the moment, and we were content to talk quietly over the welcome possibility of soon meeting relatives and friends.

The " Yankee " was destined, however, to experience a little more service before dropping anchor in home waters.

For several days we cruised along the coast between Casilda and Cienfuegos. We came to know it very well; every ravine in the mountains was familiar, every inlet in the coral-bound shore known to us. It began to grow monotonous.

"REMEMBER THE FISH."

Time lay rather heavy on our hands, but not too heavy, for we were put to work, two guns' crews at a time, coaling in a new and torrid fashion: the coal in the after hold had not all been taken out during the northern cruise, so it was decided to pack it in bags, two hundred pounds to a bag, carry it forward and stack it in an unused ballast tank.

Number Six and Number Eight guns' crews were among the first to engage in this pleasant occupation.

We found heat enough below to supply a good-sized house all winter, so clothing seemed unnecessary. We stripped to the waist, "Cumming," a member of Number Six gun's crew, remarking that he thought a cool glance and a frozen smile would be sufficient in such a warm climate.

The work was hard and dirty and the heat terrific. We saw no necessity for the transfer. Jack never can see the need of work unless it happens that some other crew is doing it.

We cheered ourselves, however, by singing "There's a hot time in the old ship to-day."

While we lay close inshore, the "Dixie" cruised outside, and toward evening the two vessels met, and together we went to Casilda, a port near Trinidad. We stood by while the

"Dixie" threw a few shells into the fort. Two days later the "Yankee" parted from her consort and proceeded to the Isle of Pines.

It was here one of the most laughable incidents of the cruise occurred. While steaming past one of the outlying islands, a small fleet of fishing sloops was discovered at anchor inshore. Under ordinary circumstances such unimportant craft would not have been molested, but in the present case it was suspected that they formed part of the fleet supplying fish to the Havana market. To destroy them was our bounden duty.

"Man the starboard fo'c'sle six-pounder and fire a shell in their direction," ordered the captain from the bridge.

The gun was loaded in short order, and presently a projectile went screeching across the water, dropping with a splash near the largest sloop. Several small rowboats were seen to pull away from the smacks, and it was evident the crews had fled in terror. Directly after dinner, the "Yankee's" first cutter and the second whaleboat were ordered away, manned and armed. A Colt machine gun was placed in the bow of the former, and each carried an extra squad of armed marines.

When the expedition returned it had in tow

"REMEMBER THE FISH."

five decked sloops, one of which contained a quantity of fresh fish. Orders were given to attach the latter to our stern, and to fire the others and set them adrift. Before this was done, however, enough fish to supply the wardroom and cabin messes were taken out.

"The crew can have its share to-morrow," quoth the captain.

The "crew" waited impatiently, but when the morrow came it was found that, through some one's blunder, the sloop containing the fish had been burned, and an empty one towed to sea with us. The joke, if it might be so termed, was on the crew.

The watchword heretofore on the "Yankee," as on every one of Uncle Sam's ships, had been "Remember the Maine." Hereafter it was "Remember the fish." This was done so persistently that the officer who was responsible for the blunder was dubbed "Fish," and whenever he went near any member of the crew he was likely to hear, in a low tone, "Remember the fish."

After leaving the Isle of Pines the eastern shore of Cuba was rounded and a straight run made for Key West. At noon on the 27th of June, just twenty-nine days after the "Yankee" sailed from New York, we again entered a home port. The time was brief as time goes, but our varied experiences in foreign waters made the sight of the stars and stripes flaunting over American soil particularly pleasing.

As we neared our anchorage the most entrancing rumors were rife. We were to get shore liberty without doubt, and the ship was to be coaled by outside labor. We took no stock in the latter rumor till an officer voiced it—then we believed. Our clean blues were furbished up, lanyards scrubbed, and money counted. We understood that there was little to see at Key West; that it was a dull and uninteresting place. Still it was land, and we had not set foot ashore for almost three months.

If we had not been so anxious to get ashore we might have been able to appreciate the marine picture.

The harbor, if it could be called a harbor, was full of war vessels, prizes, and colliers. Three grim monitors tugged at their anchor chains, apparently impatient at the restraint, while a few graceful, clean-cut, converted yachts swung with the tide.

The gunboat "Wilmington," and the cruisers "Newark" and "Montgomery," floated with a bored air. In ship's language they said, Why are we loafing here? Why not be up and doing?

"*REMEMBER THE FISH.*"

The "Lancaster," a fine old frigate, the flagship of the commodore, had a fatherly air and seemed to say: "Be good and you will all have a chance."

Once more we got our shore-going clothes ready, only to be disappointed, and again the promises made to us proved elusive. The day following our arrival, we were told that no shore liberty would be given at Key West, and while the reasons were all sufficient, a man who has set his mind on an outing ashore after a hundred days at sea, finds it somewhat hard to reconcile himself to the inevitable.

One of the hardest, if not the hardest, thing we had to bear was the lack of letters and news from home. When one has been deprived of all tidings from his own people for so long the longing for word of them becomes almost unbearable.

In the midst of our toughest work we felt that a letter from home would act like a strong tonic and brace us for the effort, and it would have done so. But no such balm came, though we eagerly scanned every incoming vessel for the signal "We have mail for you." Now at last, though there might be tons on tons of coal to be put in at Key West, though the ship might have to be scrubbed and painted from truck to water line, we felt certain we would get letters from home. Letters that we ached for. And so when we sighted the fleet and old fort, and realized that we had reached Key West and mail at last, our joy was too great for utterance.

The whaleboat went ashore and brought back two bags of precious missives, with the sad news that eight bags had been sent on a despatch boat to the "Yankee" at Santiago.

We were glad enough to get two bags, yet we almost gnashed our teeth when we thought of the eight fat pouches that were chasing us around the island of Cuba.

The mail was brought to the wardroom and dumped out on the table for the commissioned officers to sort and pick out their own letters. A news-hungry group stood the while at the doors, watching and mentally grumbling that such an awfully long time was being taken to accomplish so simple a thing.

Finally the master-at-arms was sent for and the worth-its-weight-in-gold mail turned over to him to distribute. To the gun deck poured the eager throng. The master-at-arms backed up against the scuttle-butt for protection, then shouted out: "Let one man from each mess get the mail; the rest of you stand off, or you won't get any till to-morrow." The rest of us stood to one side then, realizing that time would be thus saved.

"Jimmy Legs" called out the names, and the representatives of the different messes took them. We heard Kennedy's name called, and a murmur of sympathy spread around. "Poor chap," said one, "he would give the use of his wounded arm for that letter."

"Yes," said another; "he has to suffer homesickness as well as pain, and a letter from home would brace him up as nothing else could."

Every man took his treasures to a quiet place, a place apart, if such could be found, to enjoy them alone. The few who got none—well! may I never see such disappointed, sorrowful faces again.

The letters read and pondered over awhile, tongues began to be loosened, and soon all over the ship was heard the buzz of conversation. Chums told each other the little items of news that to them seemed the most important things in the world. And after all had been told and retold, the men gathered in groups and discussed their past months' experiences.

"Do you know," said Craven (a descendant of that famous line of naval heroes, a seaman and member of Number Thirteen six-pounder gun's crew), "I think we are wonderfully fortunate to come through this experience as well as we have. Just think! We have been under fire five times, and only one man has been injured. Why," he continued, and his hearers nodded assent, "I used to have the most awful visions—thought I saw the men lying round our gun in heaps, while fresh ones jumped to take the places of the fallen."

"And they would," said messenger "Hop," who happened to be passing on his way aft to deliver an order.

The "Yankee" had seen some spirited fighting, though most of her crew had anticipated nothing more exciting than patrol duty.

Moreover, it was almost certain that we had not seen the end of active service. At present, however, the crew settled down once more to the monotony of ship life in port—which is about equivalent to garrison duty for a soldier.

"SAW THE MEN LYING ROUND THE GUN IN HEAPS" (*page* 236).

"THE DECKS WERE SWABBED THOROUGHLY" (*page* 240).

CHAPTER XVII.

IN GOD'S COUNTRY.

The "Yankee's" stay in Key West was marked by one of the most melancholy incidents of the cruise. Thomas Clinton LeValley, one of the first of the New York Naval Reserves to respond to the call for volunteers, died from appendicitis in the hospital ashore, to which he had been removed for treatment. "Tom," as he was familiarly called by his shipmates, was on board the "Yankee" during the five engagements of that vessel, and proved himself loyal and steadfast on every occasion. He was well liked by the officers and men of the crew, and his death was deeply regretted by all. It was his fate to be the one member of the New York Naval Reserves to lose his life in the service of his country.

When a big barge heaped high with coal came alongside and was made fast, we began to doubt the assurances given us, that the coal would be put in by outside labor. A tug hove in sight shortly afterward that caused our gloomy faces to light up with gladness, for it carried a gang of negroes. The tug made fast to the barge, and its living cargo was soon hard at work filling the ship's bunkers.

All that afternoon we "lingered in the lap of luxury," as "Bill" put it. At six o'clock our dusky (doubly dusky) coal heavers went ashore, their labor over for the day. Though the workmen had left, the work was still to continue. The crew coaled till twelve o'clock, working in quarter watches. The following day another barge came alongside and part of the crew had to turn to and help the hired shovellers.

"So much," said "Stump," snapping his fingers, "for the officers' assurances."

Up to this time we did not *know* where we were going. Of course the "Rumor Committee" were ready with news of destinations galore. We were to return to our patrol duty, to join the Flying Squadron and threaten the coast towns of Spain, to join the blockading squadron off Havana. We were to do a dozen or more things just as probable or just as improbable.

A coal barge still lay alongside the starboard side of the ship, when a lighter appeared and made fast to the port side, loaded with express packages, parts of machinery, pipes, and bags of mail for every ship on the Santiago blockade.

"Now we will get those eight bags of mail," said a forecastle man, exultantly. And from that moment we knew we were going back to Cuba.

But like a good many people who think they know it all—we didn't.

Bunkers, holds—almost every available space, in fact, was filled with coal.

Then began the much dreaded job of painting. Stages were hung over the side, each manned by two men, and with much reluctance we began to daub the old "Yankee" with gray paint.

The men were unaccustomed to such work, though some could handle the brushes sold in "artist's materials" shops well enough, and they spattered gray paint all over themselves. It was thought easier to wash skins than jumpers, so many were decorated in wonderful fashion.

"You would make a 'professor of tattooing' wild with envy," said Greene to "Steve," as the latter appeared over the rail.

"Well, I don't know," retorted "Steve," "I am thinking of reporting you for misappropriating government property. You've got more paint on yourself than you put on the ship."

After a day and a half of dreary work we had the satisfaction of seeing the vessel's sides one uniform color from stem to stern. It was a big job for such a short time and our arms ached at the very thought of it.

The sides painted, our attention was given to the decks. They were swabbed thoroughly, first with a damp swab, and after they were entirely dry the spar deck was covered with red shellac, this being applied with a wide varnish brush. The gun deck was then taken in hand and treated in the same way.

By Saturday night the ship was as fine as a "brand new jumping-jack before the baby sucked the paint off."

Some of the men still suffered from black-and-blue spots, which, however, a little turpentine liniment would have banished.

Rumors were rife that we would be bound for New York shortly, but few believed them; the circulators themselves certainly did not, of that we felt sure.

"The idea!" said "Mourner," who, though ready to swallow most rumoristic pills, could not manage this one. "Go to New York with

"THE SPAR DECK WAS COVERED WITH RED SHELLAC"
(*page* 240).

"THE MARINES AIRED THEIR HAMMOCKS ON THE FORE-
CASTLE DECK" (*page* 244).

eighty bags of mail for the Santiago fleet! I can see us doing it."

"Taps" sounded at nine o'clock, and we were glad enough to turn in.

When all hands were called, I rubbed my eyes in astonishment, for as I glanced out of the deadlight near which my hammock swung, I saw that we were under way and well out to sea. I put on my togs in a hurry, and after lashing and stowing my "dream bag," rushed on deck.

Yes, sure enough, we were at sea.

"Stump" came and grabbed me round the waist—he could hardly reach higher. "We're bound for New York," said he. "We met the 'St. Paul' going in and the signal boys say we signalled, 'We have urgent orders to proceed to New York.' What do you think of that?" he added, breathlessly.

"With eighty bags of mail for the Santiago fleet," said I, thinking of the poor fellows who were longing with all their hearts for those same bags.

"Regular navy style," added "Stump."

Though it was hard on our friends off Santiago we could not be cast down, and the near prospect of liberty—of an opportunity to see home and friends, of again setting foot on shore—transformed the entire crew.

Everywhere could be seen smiling faces. Laughter and merry chatter filled the air, and the rollicking songs written by "Steve" and others were more in evidence than ever. The daily routine of work seemed lighter. There was no grumbling, no fault finding; even the interminable task of shifting coal was carried on with actual cheerfulness. Grimy hands and blackened faces and tired bodies were forgotten.

"There's a mighty good dinner waiting for me in the dear old house," exclaimed "Stump," unctuously. "I can sniff it afar. And say, fellows, won't we forget—for a few hours at least—that such things as reveille and scrub and wash clothes and coal humping and salt-horse exist on earth?"

"Oh, good Mr. Captain, how long will it be before we hear the welcome call, 'Shift into clean blue, the liberty party!' and find ourselves piling over the side," groaned "Hay."

"You will be glad enough to come back to your Uncle Samuel," grinned "Steve." "When your time is up you will be waiting for the boat."

"No doubt," replied Flagg. "We will be ready to complete our time of service, but there are some, if rumor speaks the truth——"

He finished with a significant wink.

He referred to the many threats of "French leave" made by certain members of the crew—threats which did not materialize except in a very few cases. The disgruntled members of the "Yankee's" crew were composed mainly of the "outside" men—men not of the Naval Reserves. Among the latter, despite the unaccustomed hardships to which they were subjected, a firm determination existed to remain until lawfully mustered out.

The trip from Key West to New York was marked by only one important incident—the celebration of the Fourth of July. It was unlike that familiar to the majority of the crew. There were no fireworks, no parades, nor bands playing the national anthem. The day opened squally, and sharp gusts of rain swept the decks. The usual routine of work was proceeded with, and it was not until eight bells (noon) that we fully realized the date. At exactly midday a salute of twenty-one guns was fired, and those of us who were super-patriotic, took off our caps in honor of the flag. That ended the ceremony.

"Never mind," said Tommy, when one of the boys bewailed the meagre celebration, "never mind, shipmate. There's a good time coming when we can whoop 'er up for Old

Glory as much as we please. Then we'll make up for to-day. We can't expect to do much under these conditions, you know."

The day following (a fine, *cool*, bright one, and how we did appreciate it!) was spent by all hands in getting the ship spick and span for the inspection of visitors, who were sure to be on hand to welcome us.

The semi-weekly ceremony of airing hammocks and bedding was indulged in. The bugler blew "hammocks," whereupon all hands lined up to receive them from the stowers. They were then unlashed on the gun deck, and inspected by the officers of the different divisions, who ordered that they should be taken up to the spar deck. The blankets and mattresses were spread wherever sun and breeze could get at them. The rail, as well as the boats, was covered with them. Red blankets flaunted in the breeze from the rigging till we resembled an anarchist emigrant ship.

The marines aired their hammocks on the forecastle deck in the neighborhood of their guns.

After an hour or two, the word was passed to "stow hammocks," and soon all was shipshape again.

This duty was performed once or twice a

"THE BLANKETS AND MATTRESSES WERE SPREAD FOR AIRING" (*page* 244).

"UNDER THE HOSE" (*page* 253).

week, the frequency depending on weather and circumstances.

Wednesday, July 6th, we passed Sandy Hook and entered New York harbor, just thirty-six days since we left it.

As we made our way up the channel, a pilot boat hailed us and told us of Sampson and Schley's glorious victory over Cervera.

Though our joy was great and our enthusiasm intense, we were greatly disappointed that we were not in at the death. We felt sure that if we had been there our skipper would have worked the old craft in near enough to have given us a shot.

We steamed on up the bay and through the Narrows, the happiest lot of Jackies afloat. The captain of every vessel we met pulled his whistle cord until the steam gave out, and the passengers cheered and waved their handkerchiefs, or whatever came handy.

The health officer passed us in a jiffy, and before eight bells struck we were safely at anchor off Tompkinsville.

It transpired that we had been sent North on account of a yellow fever scare. The health officer proved that the fear was groundless. Again we set to work cleaning, scrubbing, polishing, and painting, so by the time our friends came crowding aboard, the ship was as neat as a new pin.

The visitors—how glad we were to see them! Only one who has looked danger in the face and realized that there might never be a home-coming in this world, could understand our feelings as our relatives and friends—bless them—came aboard.

Fathers, mothers, brothers, sisters, and other fellows' sisters crowded up the gangway to greet us.

And all were welcome.

The second day after we anchored, the port watch was given shore leave of twenty-four hours. So we donned our clean blues, and for the first time since May 9th, set foot on solid ground.

As the port watch came over the side the following day, after its liberty ashore, they were met with the order "Shift into working clothes at once and get those shells below." The red ammunition flag was flying at the foremast head, and all thoughts must be given up of the good times ashore.

The starboard watch then went on liberty ashore and the port watch tackled the ammunition.

From noon till after ten, we were kept busy

storing thirteen-inch shells for the biggest guns in the navy. They weigh 1,100 pounds apiece and are dangerous things to handle, not only on account of their weight, but because of the charge of powder each carries. We also loaded eight, six, and five-inch shells into the after hold. We turned in at eleven o'clock, and were roused at 3:30 next morning to begin the same heavy work. When the starboard watch returned the following noon, we were still at it, and they, too, had to pitch in and help as soon as they could get into working clothes.

Saturday, Sunday, and Monday were spent in the same way—stowing food for Uncle Sam's mighty guns.

The thirteen-inch shells were crated in heavy planks, bound with iron; slings of rope were placed around them and they were lowered slowly into the hold. The eight, six, and five-inch shells had a lashing of tarred rope and a loop by which they might be lifted and handled.

Charges of smokeless powder for thirteen, eight, and six-inch guns, in copper canisters, were also taken aboard.

When all was stowed, we carried enough explosives to blow the water out of the bay. At half-past two on July 12th, the anchor was raised, the cat falls manned, and we bade New

York good-by once more. A brisk northeast breeze was blowing, kicking up an uncomfortable sea, and when Sandy Hook was passed it became necessary to close all ports and batten down hatches.

The rolling and pitching of the ship soon began to make things interesting on the gun deck. Immense green seas, shipped at intervals on the upper deck, sent little streams of water trickling down through openings as yet unprotected.

At evening quarters it was all we could do to stand upright. A number of men left their stations suddenly without permission, and seemed to take great interest in the sea just over the rail.

As the sun sank, the wind rose, and with it came rain—rain in sheets—the " wettest " kind of rain.

When the port watch was relieved at eight o'clock, even the veriest landsman among us could tell that the situation was becoming serious. We turned in at once, determining to get all the sleep possible in that pandemonium of sound.

The value of hammocks in a heavy sea was proved beyond all peradventure, for once we got into them and closed our eyes, we hardly realized that the ship was almost on her beam ends much of the time.

From time to time we were wakened by the crash of a mess chest, as it broke from its lashings and careened around the deck. The mess pans and pots banged and thumped. At intervals the lurching of the vessel caused a mess table with the accompanying benches to slide to the deck with a crash.

At twelve, we of the port watch were wakened from our much-interrupted rest and ordered on deck for muster.

As we slid from our hammocks we realized for the first time the fury of the storm. It was impossible to stand upright.

The old hooker rolled so, that it was impossible to keep from sliding even when one lay prone on the deck. The men on lookout had all they could do to hang on. One moment the end of the bridge would rise high in air and the next almost bury itself in the seething waters.

The wind roared, the lightning flashed, and the thunder rolled.

The dense fog hung like a curtain round the ship, so the whistle was blown incessantly.

The boatswain's mate ordered me to go forward and stand an hour's watch on the bridge. I obeyed, creeping on all fours most of the time, till I reached the opening between the deck houses. I escaped, by a hair's breadth, a sea which came over the side like a solid green wall.

The man on the port end of the bridge whom I relieved, shouted in my ear—he could not be heard otherwise—" You want to get a good hold or you'll be fired overboard in a jiffy." Then he left me.

It was the kind of a night one felt the need of companionship. I spent a lonely hour on the bridge, eyes and ears strained for signs of other vessels, face and hands stung by the pelting rain. Underlying all other thoughts was the consciousness that we carried several hundred tons of deadly explosive that might shift any moment or be ignited by a spark from a lamp and explode.

The sandbags stored about the steering gear broke loose and were heaped in picturesque confusion. The scene aft was indescribable. A quantity of débris of varying nature slid across the smooth surface of the gun deck with a rush at every roll, making navigation a difficult, if not perilous, task. Later, to add to the tumult, one man's hammock was cut down by a falling mess table, but he escaped serious injury.

It was not until the following morning that

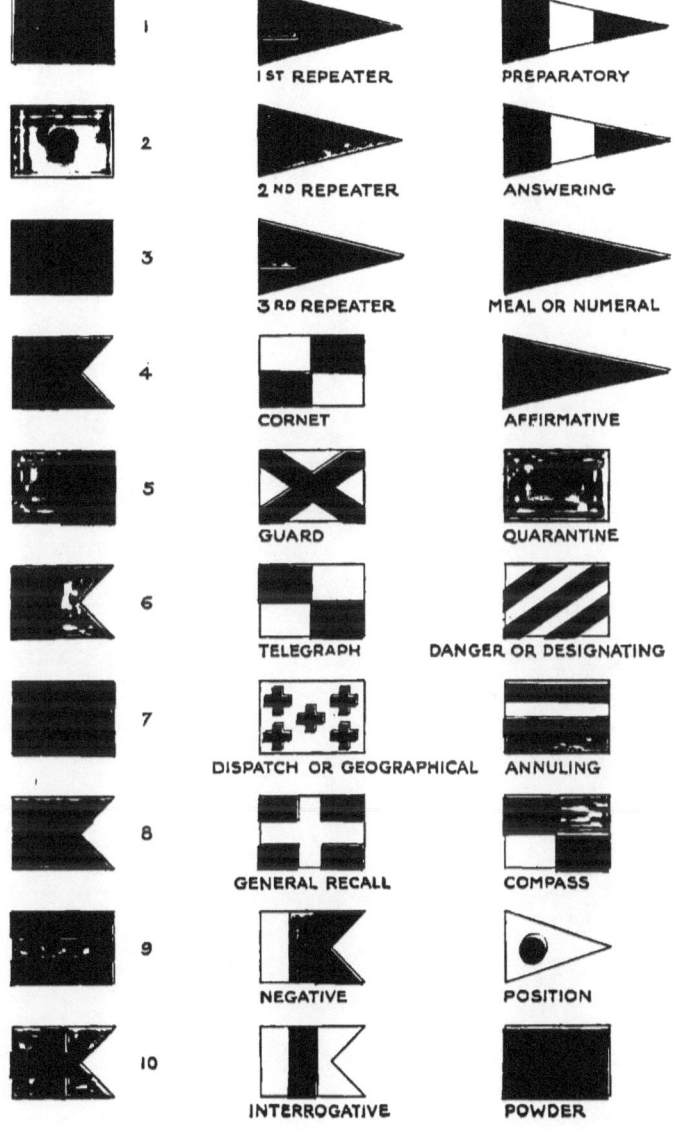

the seas subsided, but the day proved pleasant, and the mishaps of the preceding afternoon were forgotten in the excitement of reaching Norfolk, which port was reached by the "Yankee" shortly before dark. Later in the evening the ship was taken to the navy yard.

"Which means that we are going to hustle more ammunition," observed Tommy, as we made fast to a dock.

"And more stores," added "Dye."

"And coal," chimed in "Stump," with a grimace. "I am glad of it, too."

"Glad of it?" echoed "Dye," in surprise. "That's queer."

"Not at all, dear boy," was the second loader's calm reply. "D'ye see, I am in training for the billet of chief deck hand on a tramp canal boat, and this experience is just in my line."

Four days later the mooring hawsers were cast off and the "Yankee" steamed out between the capes en route to Santiago. From the hour we left Norfolk until the sighting of the Cuban coast, our time was taken up with drills of every description. The following extract from the log for July 18th, will suffice for an example:

"Cleared ship for action at three bells along with general quarters. General quarters again half an hour after turn to at noon. Fire drill and abandon ship at three bells in the afternoon. General quarters again at two bells (9 p.m.)."

Under date of July 19th, one of the crew states in his private diary: " Clear ship for action again. This is a very pretty drill, and is much liked by the boys, as it includes sending all the mess gear and provisions below, where most of them are usually 'pinched.' Clear ship for action always means an exchange of undesirable mess gear, such as broken benches, tables, etc. General quarters at 1:30; fired two shots at an invisible target with smokeless powder. Great success, this new powder. If we had only been provided with it before, every living Spaniard would have trembled at the word ' Yankee ' ! "

" What are we doing all this clear ship, general quarters, fire drill, and such business for? " said a forecastle man to Craven, who, besides being on a deck gun, from which all that was occurring on the bridge could be seen, was a messenger.

" Why, don't you know? " said the latter. " We have a war artist aboard, and all this extra drilling is being done for his special benefit, so he can work it up for his paper, I suppose."

" Well, if we ever get that artist aboard the old ' New Hampshire ' we will teach him a few things, so he can describe them from actual experience," said "Hod" the husky. "He'll be able to describe scrub and wash clothes, sweeping decks, washing dishes, and all the rest, most vividly," he continued, vindictively. "We'll show him how we get under the hose in the morning. Oh, we'll have a bully time with him, and I'll wager that when we're through the honors of naval battles will seem too trivial for him to draw!"

CHAPTER XVIII.

THE "YANKEE" ARRIVES OFF SANTIAGO.

On the twenty-first of July the "Yankee" arrived off Santiago. The "Brooklyn" was the only warship on guard, and the absence of that grim line of drab-colored ships changed the whole appearance of the coast. The "Brooklyn" seemed lonely, though she rode the seas proudly. "See," she seemed to say, "I am monarch of all I survey"; and she looked every inch a queen, as she swayed slowly in the long ground swell, her ensign snapping in the brisk breeze and Admiral Schley's flag standing out like a board. From our proximity to the shore we were enabled to obtain a better view than before. Old Morro Castle, perched above the mouth of the channel, seemed battered and forlorn. The Stars and Stripes floated on high exultingly from the very staff that formerly bore the Spanish colors, and we thrilled when we saw it. The wreck of the "Reina Mercedes" could be plainly made out, and beyond her could also be seen the masts and stack of the "Merrimac"—a monument to American heroism.

With the U. S. S. "Yankton" (which had run out of coal) in tow, we proceeded to Guantanamo. While entering the bay, the first fleet of transports bearing troops for the invasion of Porto Rico was encountered. Inside the harbor a vast squadron of American ships lay at anchor—some forty vessels in all. The spectacle of such a mighty fleet bearing our beloved colors was indeed inspiring.

We found the "Iowa," "Massachusetts," "Indiana," "Oregon," "Texas," "New York," "Marblehead," "Detroit," "Newark," "Porter," "Terror," "Gloucester," the repair ship "Vulcan," several despatch boats and colliers in the bay. Two gunboats and several steamers captured at Santiago also bore the American colors.

Such a fleet many an important port has never seen, and in New York harbor would draw immense crowds. Here the spectacle was wasted on unappreciative Cubans.

The bay presented a lively appearance with the innumerable little launches and despatch boats darting about from ship to ship. Vessels went alongside sailing colliers to have their bunkers replenished; other ships entered or left at all hours; signals were continually flying from the flagship; occasionally a Spanish launch bearing a flag of truce would come down from the town, and in the midst of it all the crews of the different men-of-war worked on in the accustomed routine, as if peace and war, drills and fighting, were all a part of man's ordinary existence.

Over a month ago we had sailed into this harbor with the "Marblehead"; the ship cleared for action, the crews at their loaded guns, and the battle ensigns flying from fore and mainmast, as well as from taffrail. This time we entered the bay with a feeling that we were to take part in a great naval spectacle.

As soon as we joined the fleet we became amenable to fleet discipline. All orders for routine work came from the flagship. "Quarters" were held but twice a day instead of three times, and then they were short and, therefore, sweet.

Each morning at eight o'clock, when a war vessel is in port, the bugler plays "colors," while the drummer beats three rolls; those of the crew who are under the open sky stand at attention, silent, facing aft, where the flag is being hauled slowly to its place. At the completion of the call all hands salute; then the work is carried on. It is a beautiful ceremony.

THE "YANKEE" ARRIVES OFF SANTIAGO.

Saluting the "colors" morning and evening is not merely a mark of respect for the Government of the nation, but is an act of worship to the God of nations—a silent prayer for guidance and care and an expression of thankfulness.

Shortly after "colors" the morning following our arrival at Guantanamo, orders were given to "turn to" on the ammunition. Launches and barges from other warships came alongside, and the charges of powder and the shells were transferred to them.

When this cargo of deadly explosive began to come aboard a "magazine watch" was set. The ammunition was stowed in all parts of the ship—forward, main, and after holds were filled. A watch was set on each of the holds. It was their duty to watch the temperature day and night and to report the same to the officer of the deck every half hour. Extreme care was taken to guard against fire. In case fire was discovered, it was the duty of the man on watch to run and turn on the water—the key for the valve which regulated this being always carried on his wrist. Then he must notify the officer of the deck, shouting "fire" as he went, after which he must go back and with the hose endeavor to put out the blaze.

Constant, wide-awake, alert watchfulness was necessary. It was hot and close below, and at night it was almost impossible to keep awake. It is difficult enough to keep wide awake for an hour's lookout on deck, when there is much to see and the air is brisk and invigorating, but it is quite a different matter to be roused in the middle of the night to stand two hours' watch in a close, hot hold, where nothing more interesting than cases of powder and the bare, blank sides of the ship are to be seen.

At first, the knowledge that the lives of all on board and the safety of the ship herself depended on the alertness of the watch, kept us wide awake and anxious, but as time went on, it grew harder and harder to resist nature's demand for sleep; therefore, when the order was given to unload the ammunition, none were gladder than the men of the "magazine watches."

After evening mess the boatswain's mate—he got his orders from the bridge—came aft, shouting as he walked, "All you men who want to go in swimming may do so right away."

There was no doubt as to the popularity of that order. "All we men" wanted to go in swimming, and that right away. In a jiffy, white figures began to drop over the side with a splash,

"HE GOT HIS ORDERS FROM THE BRIDGE" (*page* 258).

"ALL YOU MEN WHO WANT TO GO IN SWIMMING MAY DO SO" (*page* 258).

and soon shouts of glee filled the air. The water was warm and clear as crystal, and so dense with salt that a man diving, came up like a cork. In fifteen minutes the order "Knock off swimming" was passed, and though we left the water with reluctance, obedience was prompt, lest the privilege might not again be accorded us.

After hammocks had been given out, boats hoisted—all the work of the day finished, in fact —most of the men gathered aft to hear the band of the "Oregon" play. It was a volunteer band; that is, the musicians were enlisted men, not assigned for the band. They played with vim and precision.

It was almost dark; only the ships' outlines could be made out. The red and white signal lights twinkled at intervals at the mastheads of different vessels, while beams of light showed on the still, dark water from open ports. The whole fleet lay quiet while the men listened to the strains of music from the "Oregon." It was more like the rendezvous of a cruising yacht club than a fleet of warships gathered in the enemy's country.

The music from the battleship ceased, and for a moment all was still save for the lapping of the water against the ships' sides and the splash of a fish as it leaped out of water.

Suddenly and together, a shrill piping on all the ships broke the silence, followed by the hoarse cry, "All the anchor watch to muster."

On all men-of-war at eight o'clock, the anchor watch is mustered. It consists of sixteen men—eight on duty from nine till one o'clock, the other eight from one till "all hands" at 5:30. The first part always calls its relief at one o'clock.

The mustering over, all flocked aft to hear the band again, but were disappointed, for the concert was over.

However, the men had come aft for music and music they must have in some shape.

So " Steve " the modest was dragged out, and after some persuasion sang the following to the tune of " Lou, Lou, How I Love Ma Lou." "Baron," the gunner's mate, accompanied him on the mandolin, and Eickmann, the marine corporal, helped out with his guitar.

> " 'Way down at the Brooklyn navy yard,
>   Where ships are rigged for sea,
> Three hundred little 'heroes'
>   Went aboard the old 'Yankee.'
> Oh ! we were young and foolish,
>   We longed for Spanish gore,
> And so they set us working
>   As we never worked before.

THE "YANKEE" ARRIVES OFF SANTIAGO.

CHORUS:
    "Hard-tack and salt-horse every day,
      Work, slave, for mighty little pay;
    And just before we get to sleep
      We hear the bosun pipe like this
          (Whistle),
    'Up all hammocks, all hands.'

"They turn us out each morning,
    To scrub our working clothes;
To polish guns and bright work,
    To 'light' along the hose.
To wash down decks and ladders,
    To coil down miles of rope,
To carry coal in baskets,
    To live on air and hope.

CHORUS:
    "Hard-tack and salt-horse every day,
      Work, slave, for mighty little pay;
    And when we think our work is done
    We hear the bosun pipe like this
          (Whistle),
    'Turn to.'

"Way down at Santiago,
    We fit the forts one day.
The shells were bursting o'er us,
    There was the deuce to pay.
We hid our inclination
    To run and hide below,
Because we're little 'heroes,'
    They've often told us so.

CHORUS :

"Hard-tack and salt-horse every day,
Work, slave, for mighty little pay ;
And just as all the fight was over
We heard the bosun pipe like this
(Whistle),
'Gun-deck sweepers, clean sweep fore and aft.
Sweepers, clean your spit kits.'

"One Saturday we anchored
Just off the Isle of Pines,
To load up with pineapples,
And look for Spanish signs.
We called away the cutters,
With seamen filled them up,
And captured five small sailboats,
Two Spaniards and a pup.

CHORUS :

"Hard-tack and salt-horse every day,
Work, slave, for mighty little pay ;
And when we'd like to talk it over
We heard the bosun pipe this
(Whistle),
'Pipe down.'"

"That's great!" said one and all.

"There is just time for the 'Intermezzo' before tattoo, 'Baron,'" said "Pair o' Pants," the signal boy. "Give it to us, will you?"

"Baron" obligingly complied.

The boys lay around in comfortable, though

"THE 13-INCH CHARGE OF SMOKELESS POWDER WAS LOWERED DOWN" (*page* 263).

"THE ADMIRAL WENT OVER IN OUR GIG" (*page* 268).

ungraceful, attitudes, a small but appreciative audience.

As the last high note died away the ship's bugler began that lovely call, "tattoo." We listened in silence, for though we had heard it many times, it was always a delight to us. Then, too, it meant rest (not a drug in the market by any means). Every ship's crew in the harbor, at the same moment was listening to the call blown by their own bugler.

The men tumbled below and began to prepare for the voyage to dreamland.

Five minutes later, when the sleepy "taps" sounded, the decks were almost deserted save for the hammocks, which looked like huge cocoons swung horizontally.

The following days till Sunday were spent in unloading powder and shell. The six and eight-inch charges of powder and the shell were lifted by hand and slid down chutes to the barges alongside. To handle the powder and shell for the thirteen-inch guns, steam was called into service; the thirteen-inch charges being lowered into the waiting boat, by the aid of the cargo boom and steam winch.

This work was hard and the heat trying, but it was accomplished with good grace, for we were glad to get rid of the dangerous stuff.

Sunday, after the usual inspection, several visiting lists were arranged, the most popular being that for the "Oregon." We all wanted to inspect that wonderful ship. Visiting is generally conducted on Sunday or after dark. The word is passed for those who wish to visit a certain ship to "lay aft and report to the officer of the deck." The party, all in clean clothes, are taken to the vessel designated and lined up. After being counted they are allowed to go forward, where they yarn to their heart's content until the word is given by the boatswain's mate for them to muster aft again.

The "visiting party" to Uncle Sam's bulldog was cordially received and shown all over. The great battleship was as clean and neat as a new pin. She looked as if she had just come out of her builders' hands. Paint work spotless, brass work shining, engines fairly dazzling in their brightness. The crew contented and full of enthusiasm for their ship and commander—gallant Captain Clark!

We saw the guns that helped to lay low Cervera's splendid fleet and we saw "the men behind the guns."

Our attention was called to a Jacky sewing on a blue shirt.

"Do you see that man over there?" said our guide.

We answered "Yes."

"Well, that's the chap that blew up one of the torpedo boats."

"Is that so? Tell us about it." We gazed open-mouthed at the gunner as he sat cross-legged on the deck, sewing with all his might.

"Yes, that's the chap. You see, the Spaniard was coming in our direction, and coming like greased lightning. The six-pounders on the superstructure had not been able to stop her, and things began to be interesting——"

"Yes," we gasped, breathlessly, as he stopped to light his pipe.

"Well, as I was saying, the blooming torpedo boat came nearer and nearer, and did not seem to mind the hail of six-pounders any more than a duck does the rain. I dunno why, for she had no protection that a sixer would not penetrate.

"It got to be blamed exciting, when the officer of the division said to that feller over there, who was a captain of an eight-inch rifle, 'Try your hand at it.'

"Bill said, 'Aye, aye, sir, give me time and I'll plunk her sure.' All this time the sneaking craft was coming nearer and nearer. Bill adjusted his sight and looked and looked, but still did not fire.

"'For heaven's sake, hurry up!' said the division officer, getting nervous.

"'In a minute, sir,' said Bill. 'As soon as I get a good bead.'

"He was as cool as an ice machine, and as deliberate as an old hen, but he could shoot, so we held ourselves in as best we could and watched. After waiting for what seemed an hour, Bill pulled the lanyard and the old gun roared. As soon as the smoke cleared away, we looked to see the result of the shot. There was some wreckage floating where the torpedo boat had been—that was all. Bill's shot went home, and exploded in the boiler room, and the whole craft went up in an instant."

We looked again admiringly at the man sitting there so unconcernedly, and then in obedience to the boatswain's call, went aft and aboard our cutter.

All the ammunition for the fleet was unloaded by Tuesday. We still carried a small quantity of both powder and shell for the "Massachusetts."

Tuesday afternoon we anchored alongside the sailing collier "Frank A. Palmer," and began to coal. The "Yankee's" sister ship "Prairie,"

THE "YANKEE" ARRIVES OFF SANTIAGO.

manned by the Massachusetts Naval Reserves, lay on the other side; we exchanged visits and found them good fellows, and we yarned away to our heart's content.

We had now become, in a degree, used to coaling; our muscles were hardened and some long-needed labor-saving devices had been introduced, so the work was a little easier.

Coaling continued till Friday night. During the morning of that day we were told that if two hundred tons were put aboard, a chance would be given us on the morrow to see the wrecks of Cervera's once fine vessels. It was all the incentive we needed, and the coal came aboard in a steady stream. A little after seven the required amount was in the bunkers, and by eight o'clock the stages and other coaling paraphernalia were stowed away and the "Yankee" had cast loose and was anchored by herself.

The following morning dawned bright and clear. Admiral Sampson came aboard at 8:30. We manned the "cat falls" and got under way at once.

On the way down to the wrecks, the ship was cleaned, so by the time we reached the ruins of the Spanish vessels, the "Yankee" was spick and span.

We passed the wrecks of the two torpedo

boats, passed the mouth of Santiago harbor, till finally we came to the "Almirante Oquendo" and the "Maria Teresa," fifteen miles west of old Morro.

The two wrecks lay close together. They were a melancholy sight; the "Almirante Oquendo," badly listed to port, a great rent in her side, rusted, almost completely demolished. The "Maria Teresa" seemed in better shape, but many shot holes were visible in her side.

It was a dreary though gratifying sight. The great green-clothed mountains looked down serenely on these two examples of man's handiwork and man's destructiveness; the blue sea dashed itself to foam against the coral-bound coast; and the bright sun shone over all.

The admiral went over in our gig, together with the captain and executive officer. Several other boats went along, carrying, beside the regular crews, commissioned and chief petty officers.

As we watched the boats bobbing in the short billows on their way, we, who were left behind, could not help comparing these battered hulks before us with our magnificent ships in Guantanamo Bay.

All hail to the American seamen, "the men behind the guns"!

CHAPTER XIX.

HOPE DEFERRED.

For a few days there was little to do beyond the never-ending routine work: scrubbing decks, cleaning paint, and polishing bright work on guns and equipments.

We were beginning to wonder if we were to lie at anchor indefinitely, and if our last chance of seeing any active service had gone by.

On the morning of Monday, August 1st, we had orders to get under way and go to sea. Tongues began to wag at once, and before we had fairly cleared the harbor a dozen different destinations had been picked out.

It would seem as if there could be no great danger in letting the men have some knowledge of where they are bound when fairly at sea, with no beings to whom the secret might be told, save sharks and dolphins, but

"Theirs not to make reply,
Theirs not to reason why."

The navy has little use for Jacky's brains; only his trained muscles and sinews. There is no life that can be depended upon to take the pride of intellect out of a man like that of a sailor, as Rudyard Kipling has shown in the case of Harvey Cheyne. We of the crew could think of many a cad on whom we would like to try the discipline.

The most popular rumor ran to this effect: we are bound for Porto Rico to take part with the "Massachusetts," "New Orleans," "Dixie," and other ships of the fleet in a bombardment of San Juan.

By the time land had faded from view, we knew that we really were bound for Porto Rico, but for what purpose we knew not. The rumor was correct in part, at least.

We were glad to get to sea again. There is an undefinable feeling of relief, almost of joy, when the regular throbbing of the engines begins and the ship rolls and heaves to the swell.

The spirits of the men rise; smiles lighten up their faces, and snatches of song can be heard as they work coiling down lines, lashing movables, and preparing the vessel for the rough-and-tumble conflict with the sea.

As the sun sank, the waves rose. By the time

the first night watch went on duty, the old steamer was tossing like a chip.

The guns' crews of the watch on deck were ordered to sleep by their posts, and all was in readiness for instant action.

At eleven o'clock we were roused by the call for "general quarters," and in a minute all hands were in their places. We looked vainly, at first, for the cause of this commotion, but finally made out off our port bow the dim outlines of a steamer.

It was only when our ship was on the top of the roll that we could make out our chase at all— nothing but a wall of water could be seen when we lay in the trough.

"That boat is certainly doing her best to get away," said "Bill." "And, holy smoke! see how she rolls."

"She can't trot in our heat," said "Dye." "We're gaining on her every minute."

"She's not a warship," said "Long Tommy," who was lucky enough to possess a pair of glasses. "I wonder if we're going to get a prize at last?"

"You forget the fishing sloops. 'Remember the fish,'" laughed "Hay."

The two vessels came nearer and nearer, till finally they were within hailing distance.

"What ship is that?" called out Captain

Brownson, through the megaphone. "And where are you bound?"

The answer came faintly over the tossing waves: "The 'Burton,' with coal for Santiago from Guadeloupe."

"Ah, ha!" said Tommy, "we get a prize at last."

"Wait a minute," said "Stump," "he is saying something else."

A gust of wind came at that moment and carried most of the sound away, but we gathered that our hoped-for prize had papers from our consul allowing her free passage.

There was a universal groan of disappointment, and when the order was given to "secure," the hose was pulled up with unnecessary violence, hatches were lowered, and gun closets closed with no gentle hands. Such keen disappointment must somehow find a vent.

There was great excitement the following afternoon when the word was passed for all hands to get out their leggings and to wear shoes to midday quarters. And when we were arranged into companies, and had haversacks, canteens, and knapsacks doled out to us, we concluded that a landing party would be made up for Porto Rico.

"The 'old man' is going to show the 'Spin-ache' that the 'Yankee' boys can fight on land as well as on sea," said Tommy, as he yanked at an obstinate haversack strap.

We marched round and round the spar deck to the music of bugle and drum till we got well into the swing of it, and felt very martial and formidable indeed.

The "Dixie" hove in sight at this juncture, and after a long megaphone conversation, we learned that the "Massachusetts," for which we had some ammunition, was on her way to Guantanamo, so we reluctantly turned around and retraced our way, the "Dixie" leading. Porto Rico was not for us. Alas!

We felt like

"The King of France and his hundred thousand men
Drew their swords and put them up again."

The next morning we hove-to a Norwegian steamer, the "Marie," and before we realized what was being done, we found that we had a prize at last. A snug little steamer she was, well loaded down with coal for Cervera's fleet.

"Cutlets" went over in a whaleboat, with a prize crew of six men.

"Well, well! this is almost too good to be true," said an after guard. "This *is* great luck.

We capture a prize and get rid of 'Cutlets' at the same time."

To which we all said, Amen.

We separated from the "Marie," and, as the "Yankee" was much the faster, she was soon lost to sight.

The anchor had no sooner been dropped in Guantanamo Bay than our captain went over to the "New York," and then signals began to be displayed, and soon after all hands were hauling on the "cat falls."

The skipper returned; the gig was pulled up to its place, and very soon we were ploughing the water in the open. As we went out, our prize came in.

It seems the encounter with the "Burton" was told to the admiral, and he at once ordered us to go out and get her.

We headed straight out. The black smoke poured out of the funnels; the ship shook with the pounding of the strained engines. The land faded from view.

About two o'clock we sighted the object of our chase, and it only required a blank shot from the forward six-pounder to bring her to.

The prize crew, consisting of six seamen, some firemen and engineers, and officered by Lieutenant Duncan, went over and took possession of our second prize in one day.

Captor and captive then turned and headed for Guantanamo.

The men were in high spirits. Speculation was rife as to the amount of prize money each would secure, and some even went so far as to plan the spending of it.

Every one felt very gay, and as if something should be done to celebrate our good fortune. We would have liked to spend some money for an entertainment, but that was impossible.

"Dick," however, was impressed into service to furnish some amusement. "Dick," a forecastle man, is a born story-teller, and we knew if we could get him started, some fun would be assured.

After some pressure he acquiesced, and began the following yarn:

"One day a certain Irishman, Mike Dooley by name, departed this life. He was much respected, and his death caused no little sorrow to his friends and neighbors. His wife and children were simply inconsolable. The widow wished to have a handsome funeral in his honor and spent her savings in furtherance of that plan. She had enough money for everything, except the silver inscription plate. But that difficulty was easily overcome, for ' What's the matter wid Pat Molloy painting it nately in white paint?' she said.

"Pat, being approached on the subject, expressed his entire willingness, and soon after called for the casket and took it away. He was told to letter the following, in neat, white letters: ' Michael Dooley departed this life in his prime, at the age of twenty-eight.'

"Pat was a bricklayer by trade, and painting was only a ' side line ' with him.

"He started to put the inscription on the casket, and got along bravely till he came to ' age of twenty-eight.' Then he realized that he could not make the figures. He puzzled over it a long while, for he did not like to ask and thus show up his ignorance.

"Finally a bright idea struck him. Four sevens make twenty-eight—why not put down four sevens—that was easy!

"The job was finished just in time.

"The relatives and friends were gathered round to pay their last respects. One friend was asked to get up and make a few remarks. He did so and began as follows:

"' I am glad to be able to say a few words on this sad occasion, a few words of praise for our beloved friend; for other words than praise could not be said of him. I am proud to have known him and to have been numbered among his friends. His virtues need hardly be repeated. You knew him well. His generosity, his friendliness, and all the rest he possessed. I knew him from his youth up, and I am well aware of his goodness, as are you. He was a good husband, a good father, and a good friend. It is hard to give him up, but it must be. He died at the age of——'

"Here the speaker glanced at the casket beside which he stood, and read the following:

> MICHAEL DOOLEY
> DEPARTED THIS LIFE IN HIS PRIME,
> AT THE AGE OF
> 7777.

"'Yis, my bereaved friends,' he continued, 'he was a good father, husband, and friend, and none knows that better than I. He was cut off in the pride of manhood, you might say—in his prime, at the age of——'

"He glanced at the inscription again, then, after a painful pause, blurted forth: 'Well, how the divil did he escape the flood?'"

The sound of "tattoo" interrupted our laughter at this point, and all hands tumbled below.

The following day we got rid of the last of the ammunition to the "Massachusetts." A sigh of relief and thankfulness went up as the last charge of powder was taken over the side.

The same day we saw some of our prize money vanish into thin air. The "Burton" was released, and steamed out of the harbor.

It was about this time that a well-authenticated rumor went the rounds to the effect that we were to go with a formidable fleet to Spain, harass her coasts, and do up Camara's fleet. This rumor was so well founded that many of us believed it, and, consequently, much time was spent in writing farewell letters.

The prospect of soon seeing the "land of the free and the home of the brave" was not very bright. The consensus of opinion at this time was that we would see our year out in Uncle Sam's service.

There was considerable gloom. The start once made and the "Yankee" actually on her way to the land of the Dons, all would be well and all hands would be cheerful; but the contemplation of the long trip in the wrong direction was a very different matter.

The air was full of rumors. All was uncertain. We continued to write farewell letters, while the invading fleet still lay quietly at anchor, but ready to sail to the ends of the earth at a few hours' notice.

The night of August 10th was moonless and dark. There had been no music from the "Oregon's" band, and none of our men felt inclined to sing.

The uncertainty had begun to tell, and all were a little depressed.

I was "it" for anchor watch, and, as is often the case, the anchor watch manned the running small boat.

We visited several vessels of the fleet, the crew staying in the boat while the officers went aboard. When we finally started to return to our own ship, we carried two of our officers, Mr. Duncan, Mr. Barnard, and an officer from the "Indiana." As we cleared the wall-like sides of the "St. Paul," we noted that the general signal call (four red lights) was up on the "New York." Then, as we watched, the red and white bulbs began to spell out a message that made us all thrill with joy. The interest of the moment broke down all barriers of rank, and officers and men spelled out the exciting words aloud.

A-S-S-O-C-I-A-T-E-D   P-R-E-S-S   D-E-S-P-A-T-C-H
S-T-A-T-E-S   T-H-A-T   P-E-A-C-E   P-R-O-T-O-C-O-L
H-A-S   B-E-E-N   A-G-R-E-E-D   U-P-O-N.

We Jackies would have liked to yell, but our lessons had been too well learned, and we restrained ourselves. We put the officer from the "Indiana" aboard his own ship and then returned to the "Yankee."

As soon as the boat was secured for the night, I went around waking some of my particular friends to tell them the great news, forgetting that they could see it quite as well as I. All were too good-natured, however, to object; on the contrary, they seemed glad to talk about it. There was some dispute as to the meaning of the word "protocol"; but all agreed that, whatever its meaning, it must be good, coupled as it was with "peace."

As we talked quietly, we heard faintly, softly, a verse of "Morse's" song:

> "Our fighting cruise will soon be o'er,
>   Hurrah! Hurrah!
> We'll be happy the moment our feet touch shore,
>   Hurrah! Hurrah!
> And 'Cutlets' and 'Hubbub' and all the rest
> May stick to the calling they're fitted for best,
> But *we'll* all feel gay when
>   The 'Yankee' goes sailing home."

In spite of the peace news we got orders to go out with the "Dixie" and blockade the Crooked Island Passage. So about four o'clock we hauled up the anchor and went to sea. All were gay, and many shook their hands in farewell to Guantanamo Bay.

We were instructed to keep a sharp lookout for the steamer "Monserrat," which had gained fame as a blockade runner. It was rumored that she carried Captain-General Blanco; that she was well armed, and had a captain noted for his unscrupulousness and for his fighting qualities.

"I'd like to meet that ship," said "Hay," "have a good 'scrap' with her, get a couple of shot holes in our upper works and battle flags, and then bring her triumphantly into Key West or, better still, New York."

"Want to go out in a blaze of glory, do you?" said Tommy, the long.

"Sure. I'd like to burn some of that powder we took such trouble to load."

This expressed the sentiments of the whole ship's company.

To have one more good fight—in which we were to come out victorious, of course—get a few souvenir shot holes where no harm would be done, and then go home. This would just about have suited us.

We floated around lazily all day Friday and Saturday with a chip on our shoulder, as it were, but no "Monserrat" came to knock it off.

The lookouts at the masthead strained their eyes, and half the men not actually at work did likewise. All in vain; not an enemy did we see. A number of transports homeward bound, bearing worn but happy soldiers, were passed, and some came near enough to exchange cheers and good wishes.

The screw revolved but slowly, and the ship moved just enough to give steerage way. Every passing wave did as it wished with the great hulk, and she rolled like a log in the long swell.

Sunday night a change came over the almost quiet ship. The propeller turned with some energy; the steering engine whirred, and the "Yankee" changed her course. This time she headed straight for Guantanamo, and before many minutes we knew that we were returning to our old anchorage. The orders were to blockade the passage and keep a bright lookout for the "Monserrat"; if by Sunday at six o'clock she had not appeared, we were to return to the fleet.

The men who were so sure that we should never see Guantanamo again wore a sheepish air, and those who were not so sure lorded over them and remarked cheerfully, "I told you so."

Those of us who were sleeping at midnight were wakened and told to come to the port and look. Sleepily we obeyed, but the moment we reached the opening we were wide awake. There, not three miles off, rolling in the ground swell, lay a great fleet, the searchlights sweeping the heavens and sea; the signal lanterns twinkling.

As we looked, we saw at the masthead of the foremost vessel the signal lights spell out A followed by D, the "Yankee's" private night signal. Then, and our eyes almost started from our heads as we gazed, the lights continued to spell:

"Blockade raised; hostilities ceased."

"Hurrah!" shouted some one behind me.

"Wait a minute," said "Hay," "that's not all."

The lights went on spelling: "We are on our way to New York. You are to proceed to Guantanamo."

The hurrah, as we spelled out the first sentences, was followed by a groan, as we read the last. We were glad, indeed, to know that peace had come, but it was hard to see that great fleet homeward bound, and know that we must go back to our old post, to stay indefinitely.

"Hope deferred maketh the heart sick."

CHAPTER XX.

TAPS.

The days following our arrival at Guantanamo were days of keen expectation and equally keen disappointment. A rumor that we were to return home at once would start up from nowhere in particular, and circulate until it was believed. Then would come a denial and consequent discontent. The enforced idleness of riding at anchor day after day became so monotonous at last, that any little incident served to create excitement. Visiting parties between the ships were permitted occasionally, and the "Yankee's" crew grasped the opportunity to inspect some of the other auxiliary cruisers. One or two liberty parties were allowed ashore at Camp McCalla, from which the men returned, tired and warm, but full of enthusiasm and interest for the things they had seen. The amount of "curios" and souvenirs brought aboard would fill a museum. Pieces of projectiles and Mauser cartridge shells, fragments of an unusual red wood, and pieces of fossil rock, of which the cliff was composed, were stowed away in bags and ditty boxes.

The bay now had a very deserted appearance. All the battleships and many of the cruisers had gone North. The auxiliary cruisers, "New Orleans," "Newark," "Marblehead," and a number of converted yachts were all that remained, besides our own vessel. It was still a goodly fleet, but in comparison to the great squadron, seemed small.

For the first time we were at a loss for something to do. Time hung heavy on our hands. The routine work, including morning "quarters," was finished by half-past ten every morning, and the balance of the day was spent as pleased us best, within certain well-defined limits.

Much time and thought were spent in chasing down rumors, and watching signals from the flagship.

Troopships from Santiago, laden with homeward-bound troops, sailed by the mouth of the harbor, but we, the first volunteers to reach the seat of war and to see active service, still lingered. The "Resolute" and "Badger" left at last, and it was rumored that we would follow next day. But still we lingered.

Occasionally we got mail that told of home doings, and almost every letter finished with, "I suppose that you will soon be home, now that peace is declared." But still we lingered.

We knew that we could hardly expect to be relieved at once; that there were many arrangements to be made in the Navy Department; many orders to be signed, and new plans to be formulated. But the thought carried little comfort with it. The pangs of homesickness were getting a strong hold on us.

Dr. " Gangway " McGowan had the ship's carpenter nail a nice, smooth piece of board over a hole in the wire netting of his cabin door; some wag took advantage of the opportunity, and lettered plainly the following, on its white surface:

Dr. " GANGWAY " McGOWAN.

Office Hours:	Specialty: Cold
All hands to	feet and home-
hammocks.	sick " heroes."

He would have done a rushing business if he could have found a sure cure for homesick " heroes."

On Tuesday, August 23d, our depression reached its culminating point, for the word had been passed unofficially that we might lay here indefinitely—two weeks, a month, three months

—there was no telling when we would get away from what had become a hateful spot to us. The men went about with a dejected air, and while all were good-natured enough, there was little inclination to talk.

As night drew near, we saw several troopships pass the harbor homeward bound, and the sight did not lighten our gloom.

When the sun finally sank, we were as melancholy a crowd as ever trod a deck.

The men gathered in little groups, bewailing in monosyllables the decidedly gloomy future, when some one glanced up and saw that Commodore Watson's flagship, the "Newark," was showing the general signal lights. Then, as the answering lights blazed on the other ships, the red and white lanterns began to spell out a message.

The news spread at once that the flagship was signalling a general message or one of interest to the whole fleet.

Soon the rail was lined with signal boys, and signal boys, *pro tem*.

Those who could read them, spelled the messages aloud, letter by letter.

"'Y-A-N-K-E-E' A-N-D 'N-I-A-G-A-R-A' W-I-L-L S-A-I-L F-O-R T-O-M-P-K-I-N-S-V-I-L-L-E T-O-M-O-R-R-O-W. 'D-I-X-I-E' A-N-D 'F-E-R-N' W-I-L-L G-O T-O H-A-M-P-T-O-N R-O-A-D-S."

With a single bound all was changed from gloom to gladness.

No man could say how glad he was, but every man felt his heart grow warm within him. There was a deep feeling of gratitude for the providential care we had received, and for the happy release that now had come.

"Cupid," the ship's bugler, played "Home, Sweet Home," and instead of mobbing him as we would have done had he played it three hours earlier, we applauded. He also played "America," and then "Dixie," in honor of our Maryland friends on our sister ship of that name. It pleased them mightily, as was evidenced by the cheer that came over the quiet water to us. Their bugler returned the compliment soon after by playing "Yankee Doodle."

There was much good feeling when the men went below, to turn in, but not to sleep; we were too happy for that.

As the talk and laughter gradually died down (the order, "Turn in your hammocks and keep silence," was not very strictly observed that night), a voice would be heard singing—not always the same voice:

"But we'll all feel gay when
    The 'Yankee' goes sailing home."

The following morning Scully did not have

"SANG OUT AS HE HEAVED THE LEAD" (*page* 289).

"EIGHT BELLS"

to repeat " up all hands," for he had hardly got the words out of his mouth before every man was scrambling into his clothes as fast as he could.

Soon after breakfast the order was given to hoist up the catamaran, and then the rest of the boats were pulled up one by one. The boat's falls were run away with in a fashion that made the officers smile. The tackle-blocks fairly smoked.

The only thing that marred our perfect joy was the departure of some of the marines to the "New Orleans." We had grown to like them all very much, and especially a pleasant fellow we dubbed " Happy," because of his unvarying cheerfulness. We had hoped to bring them all back with us, and were sorry to see them go.

We listened with eager ears for the final order before sailing, " All hands on the cat falls," and just before noon we heard it. In ready response the men came tumbling up, and in a jiffy the anchor was pulled up as if it weighed five hundred, instead of five thousand pounds.

The leadsman stood on his little platform and sang out, as he heaved the lead, the number of fathoms. It was the last touch we had of Cuban soil.

As the old ship gathered headway, cheer after cheer rang out from the ships that were left behind, and in answer to each our crew, which had gathered on the forecastle, gave three rousing hurrahs and a tiger.

So we sailed out of Guantanamo Bay for the last time.

It was with a feeling of sadness mixed with joy that we watched the headland, that stands like a guard on one side of the bay, disappear in the haze. We were one of the first ships to enter its then hostile portals. We had gained renown there; we had seen the American flag raised on its beautiful shores, and but a few minutes ago we heard a ringing American cheer come over its clear waters, bidding us Godspeed and a joyful home coming.

The voyage home was like a triumphal journey. All hands were in high spirits. The gloom of a few hours before was dispelled by the talismanic words, "'Yankee' and 'Niagara' will sail for Tompkinsville."

Though we were exceedingly glad, there was a good deal of quiet thinking going on.

One and all realized that we had been exposed to no ordinary dangers. Danger from the enemy's fire; danger from a deadly climate; danger from the effects of unaccustomed labor; danger from wind and raging sea. We had been brought through safe and sound by an all-wise God to lead peaceful, useful, and, it is hoped, helpful lives at home.

This same thought had been in our minds many times before, and with the feeling of thankfulness would come a sense of surprise that we should pass through it all without harm.

We sped on and on, the ship's prow ever pointed North. We watched the water to note the change in color; to see when the blue water of the Gulf Stream should be left behind and the green northern sea should be entered.

As we neared New York our impatience grew with every added mile, and this eagerness was felt by officers as well as men.

We sometimes forgot that our officers were capable of feeling disappointment, impatience, and joy; that they also had to stand watch and get along on short allowance of sleep; that they, too, were subject to annoyances as well as we. If we had not felt this before, we fully realized, now, how much *our* officers had done for us.

Lieutenants Duncan, Greene, and Barnard, Dr. McGowan, Ensigns Dimock and Andrews, always treated us fairly and honestly.

Every man has a deep-seated feeling of loyalty and affection for them that will last as long as life shall last.

As the tropical latitudes were left astern the

nights became cool, and the watch on deck had the novel experience of walking post in pea coats. Shortly after daybreak on the twenty-seventh of August the Atlantic Highlands were sighted, and, to quote one of the forecastle men, "All hands shouted to see God's country once more!"

Though we had seen the Highlands, Sandy Hook, and all the familiar landmarks of the harbor many times, never had they seemed so attractive.

The steam vessels we met tooted a welcome, as our identity became known, and the sailing craft dipped their colors in salute.

Inside the Narrows, and ranged along the Staten Island shore, we found our companions of the Santiago blockade, and, as we passed through the fleet to our anchorage, the crew stood at "quarters" in their honor.

We heard later of the great reception these tried and true fighting ships of Uncle Sam's had received, and we only regretted that we were not present to add our little mite to the applause.

After two days' stay off Tompkinsville, during which time the ship was fairly overrun with visitors eager to see the "Yankee" and her crew of "heroes," we steamed through the Narrows en route for League Island. Orders had arrived from Washington providing for the paying off and discharge of the New York Naval Reserves, and little time was lost in obeying.

On reaching League Island, the naval station near Philadelphia, we found the old-time war monitors "Nahant" and "Jason" in port. The crew of the "Nahant," made up of the New York Naval Reserves, were in readiness to accompany the "Yankee's" crew back to the metropolis.

While waiting for the specified date—Friday, September 2d—bags were packed for the last time, and all preparations made for leaving the ship. Now that the hour for departure was rapidly approaching, many of the boys began to express regrets. Despite the hardships attending the cruise, it had brought many happy days—days made pleasurable by novel and strange surroundings—and it is not claiming too much to say that not one of the "Yankee's" crew would have surrendered his experience.

Friendships had been formed, too—friendships cemented by good fellowship and mutual peril. Those who have spent many days at sea know that acquaintances made on shipboard in the midst of calms and storms and the dangers of the deep, are lasting. And that was now being impressed upon the boys of the "Yankee."

While the crews of the "Nahant" and "Yankee" were preparing for the railway trip to New York, arrangements were being made in that city for a rousing welcome to the returning Naval Reserve Battalion.

Shortly after ten the boys were mustered aft to hear Captain Brownson's parting speech. In his usual brisk manner he said that we were now to go back to our peaceful avocations; to our homes; to join our relatives and friends, and to become again private citizens. He ended by wishing us the best of luck.

The cheers that followed shook the old ship from keel to topmast, nor were the cheers for Lieutenant Hubbard any the less hearty.

A very few minutes after, we piled into a tug and steamed away. Little was said, for there was a feeling of real regret: we were fond of the old boat, after all.

"Patt," the gunner's mate; the marines, and the few men of the engineer force who stayed on board, waved good-by.

We boarded a special train with the crew and officers of the "Nahant," and were soon speeding over the level country towards New York.

After a very fast trip we reached Jersey City, where we were fitted out with rifles and belts,

MARCHING THROUGH CITY HALL PARK, NEW YORK CITY (*page* 295).

and were met by the band that was to lead us through the city.

The people of New York turned out to give us a rousing welcome.

It was a welcome we shall never forget—a welcome that made us forget all hardships, all dangers. Whatever pride we may have had in our achievements was drowned in that thunderous greeting; we were humbled, for real heroes could hardly have deserved such a reception.

The Mayor stood in front of the City Hall and reviewed us, and later we were reviewed by the President himself, at Madison Square.

As the head of the column turned down Twenty-sixth Street, heading to our old receiving ship the "New Hampshire," the band struck up "Home, Sweet Home." The men still marched with heads erect and eyes to the front, but many of those eyes were dimmed with a moisture that almost prevented their owners from seeing the long, homeward-bound pennant that floated from the masthead of the old frigate.

As for the greeting given by mothers and sisters and relatives of every degree and by friends assembled on the "New Hampshire," that is one experience that cannot be described; it must be felt to be appreciated. Suffice it that every member of the New York Naval Battalion felt amply repaid for the hardships endured and the sacrifices made in the service of Old Glory. And if the occasion should again arise for the calling out of the Naval Reserves of the First New York Battalion, they, together with their comrades, the Naval Reserve Battalions of other cities, will cheerfully don their "clean whites" and respond to muster.

"Pipe down!"

APPENDIX.

THE NAVAL MILITIA OF THE UNITED STATES.

The Naval Militia is a volunteer organization made up of certain patriotic citizens of the United States, who conceived the idea that the country could be served by its sons as well in the naval branch of the National Defence as in the military. The subject of a naval volunteer force had been agitated for several years, but it was not until the latter part of June, 1891, that the first enlistments were made.

Since that time the success of the organization has been continuous and most gratifying, and it has required only the recent war with Spain to prove that its value to the country at large cannot be overestimated. At the outbreak of hostilities, the strength of the Naval Militia throughout the country was 4,445 officers and enlisted men, but the rush of recruits incidental to the opening of the war vastly increased that number.

The scope of the organization is naturally limited to those States bordering on the seacoast and the Great Lakes, but the interest taken in it to-day by the people is widespread and emphatic. The existence of this interest was amply proved by the enthusiastic welcome tendered the returning crews of the "Badger," "Dixie," "Prairie," "Yosemite," and "Yankee" by the citizens of the cities more closely concerned, and by the country at large.

A GUNNER ABOARD THE "YANKEE."

In a report made to Secretary Long in 1897 by Theodore Roosevelt, then Assistant Secretary of the Navy, these prophetic words were used :

"The rapidity with which modern wars are decided renders it imperative to have men who can be ready for immediate use, and outside of the regular navy these men are only to be found in the Naval Militia of the various States. If a body of naval militia is able to get at its head some first-class man who is a graduate of Annapolis ; if it puts under him as commissioned officers, warrant officers, and petty officers men who have worked their way up from grade to grade, year after year, and who have fitted themselves for the higher positions by the zeal and painstaking care with which they have performed their duties in the lower places ; and if the landsmen, ordinary seamen, and seamen go in resolutely to do real work and learn their duties so that they can perform them as well as the regulars aboard our warships, taking pride in their performance accordingly as they are really difficult—such an organization will, in course of time, reach a point where it could be employed immediately in the event of war.

"Most of the Naval Militia are now in condition to render immediate service of a very valuable kind in what may be called the second line of defence. They could operate signal stations, help handle torpedoes and mines, officer and man auxiliary cruisers, and assist in the defence of points which are not covered by the army. There are numbers of advanced bases which do not come under the present scheme of army coast defence, and which would have to be defended, at any rate during the first weeks of war, by bodies of Naval Militia ; while the knowledge they get by their incessant practice in boats on the local waters would be invaluable.

APPENDIX.

"Furthermore, the highest and best trained bodies could be used immediately on board the regular ships of war; this applies to the militia of the lakes as well as to the militia of the seacoast—and certainly no greater tribute is necessary to pay to the lake militia. Many of these naval battalions are composed of men who would not enlist in time of peace, but who, under the spur of war, would serve in any position for the first few important months."

The last sentence of the above extract is of peculiar interest, inasmuch as it proved true in every particular. The crews of the auxiliary ships manned by the Naval Militia during the Spanish-American war of 1898 were composed of men who, in civil life, were brokers, lawyers, physicians, clerks, bookkeepers, or men of independent means. They sacrificed their personal interests for the moment, and, in their patriotic zeal, accepted positions of the most menial capacity on board ship.

Prior to the outbreak of war they had entered into training with the utmost enthusiasm. The Navy Department had assigned some of the older vessels to the various naval brigades, to be used as training ships, and with these as headquarters the brigades began drilling. In addition to the regular routine, summer cruising was taken up.

The First Battalion, New York State Militia, for instance, went in a body to Fisher's Island, off the eastern end of Connecticut, and there engaged in landing parties, camping, and sham battles. On another occasion the battalion embarked on board the battleships "Massachusetts" and "Texas," each militiaman having a regular bluejacket for a running mate, and doing just as he did. The two ships cruised in the vicinity of Fisher's Island, and a programme was carried out which included instruction in the different parts of the ship in great guns and ordnance, such drills as abandon ship, arm and away boats, clear ship for action, general quarters, signalling, and in the use of torpedoes.

During one of the cruises of the Massachusetts Naval Brigade a detachment was engaged in locating signal stations on the coast from the New Hampshire State line to Cape Ann, and it was due to the efforts of this detachment that the signal stations established during the late war proved so efficient.

The Naval Militia of Maryland, Louisiana, Illinois, and other States were given opportunities for instruction in the handling of guns, the care of wounded, in infantry drill, limited artillery practice with rapid-fire batteries, and all the details of naval life, and so well did they benefit by it that the authorities at Washington announced a willingness to trust any of the warships in their sole charge.

It was to reach this pinnacle, as it may be termed, that the Naval Militia organizations of the United States had striven, and when they were finally called upon by the Government they proved their worth by boarding modern warships, doing the work of regular sailors, and fighting for their country with a degree of skill and zeal that has earned for them the commendation of their fellow-citizens.

UNITED STATES NAVAL CODE FOR VISUAL SIGNALLING.

To signal with flag or torch "wigwag":

There are but *one* position and *three* motions.

The *position* is with the flag held vertically in front of the body; the signalman facing squarely the point to which the message is to be sent.

APPENDIX.

The *first* or 1 is a motion to the right of the sender.

The *second* or 2 is a motion to the left of the sender.

The *third* or 3 : the flag is dropped in front of the sender and instantly returned to *position*.

The entire code is made up of these three motions—1, 2, and 3. Every letter begins and ends with *position*.

"WIGWAG" CODE. UNITED STATES NAVAL CODE FOR VISUAL AND TELEGRAPHIC SIGNALLING.

ALPHABET.

A........22	J.......1122	S.........212
B......2112	K......2121	T...........2
C........121	L.......221	U.........112
D........222	M......1221	V.........1222
E........12	N........11	W.......1121
F.......2221	O........21	X.......2122
G......2211	P.......1212	Y.........111
H........122	Q......1211	Z........2222
I............1	R.......211	

NUMERALS.

1..................1111	2..................2222
3..................1112	4..................2221
5..................1122	6..................2211
7..................1222	8..................2111
9..................1221	0..................2112

ABBREVIATIONS.

a........after.	n........not.	ur.....your.
b........before.	r..........are.	w......word.
c........can.	t......... the.	wi.....with.
h........have.	u........you.	y.......why.

x x 3 = " numerals follow " or " numerals end."
sig. 3 = signature.
3 = End of word.
33 = End of sentence.
333 = End of message.
22, 22, 3 = I understand.

A GUNNER ABOARD THE "YANKEE."

The complete number opposite each letter or numeral stands for that letter or numeral.

Example: The signal sent by Commodore Schley's flagship "Brooklyn" that memorable 3d of July—

T H E   E N E M Y ' S   F L E E T
2, 122, 12 3   12, 11, 12, 1221, 111, 212 3   2221, 221, 12, 12, 2, 3
L, RLL, RL D   RL, RR, RL, RLLR,RRR, LRL D   LLLR, LLR, RL, RL, L, D

I S   C O M I N G   O U T   O F
1, 212 3   121, 21, 1221, 1, 11, 2211 3   21, 112, 2 3   21, 2221
R, LRL D   RLR, LR, RLLR, R, RR, LLRR D   LR, RRL, L D   LR, LLLR

H A R B O R.
122, 22, 211, 2112, 21, 211, 333.
RLL, LL, LRR, LRRL, LR, LRR, DDD.

R = Right = 1.   L = Left = 2.   D = Drop = 3.

NIGHT SIGNALLING.

The lights in the Ardois system—named after its inventor—sometimes called "shroud lights," are placed well up on the foremast. They are red and white electric bulbs. There are four of each placed in a line one above the other, in groups of two—a red and white bulb together. Unlike the "wigwag" system, the whole letter is shown at once.

The code is the same as the "wigwag." One is indicated by a red light, two by white, and three by the combination, white, white, red and white.

Both systems may be mastered very easily by a little painstaking practice, and much amusement may be had through the mystification of those who do not understand it. A "wigwag" flag may be easily made by sewing a white square of muslin in the centre of a red bandana handkerchief.

The best method of learning this system is to send simple messages, looking up the letters that there is any doubt about, and correcting mistakes as you go along.

APPENDIX.

NAVY CODE FLAGS.

Messages sent by the navy code flags cannot be read except by the aid of the code book. There are ten numeral flags—1 to 9, and one for 0. All messages are made up by means of these ten flags headed by the code flag (whether it be geographical, telegraph, or navy list).

For instance, a line of bunting is sent up on the flagship's signal halliards. It is read from the top down. The geographical flag flies first; then follow 7, 6, 3, 8. It means that the message can be found in the geographical list, number 7638.

The repeaters are used to avoid confusion. Instead of putting two number 1 flags together, for instance, number 1 is flown with a repeater under it; second repeater repeats number 2, and so on.

PREPARATORY.—Over hoist. Prepare to execute subjoined order.

INTERROGATION.—Alone. What is that signal? or "I don't understand—repeat." Above hoist puts signal in interrogative sense.

ANSWERING.—Flown by ship receiving message indicates that signal is understood.

AFFIRMATIVE.—Alone. Yes. Above hoist puts message in affirmative or permissive sense.

NEGATIVE.—Alone. No. Above hoist puts message in negative sense.

MEAL or NUMERAL.—Alone. Crew at mess. Above or below hoist—the numeral flags are to be taken as numbers simply.

CONVOY.—Alone at fore, means naval convoy. Above hoist means use navy list.

A GUNNER ABOARD THE "YANKEE."

POSITION.—In manœuvres, hoisted by each ship as it gets into position ordered; lowered when next ship gets into place.

GUARD or GUIDE.—As its name implies—flown by guard or guide ship.

TELEGRAPH.—Use telegraph list.

DESPATCH or GEOGRAPHICAL.—Alone at fore, indicates that the ship flying it is carrying despatches. Above hoist. Use geographical list.

CORNET.—Alone. Ship about to sail. Over number. Official number of ship.

GENERAL RECALL.—Recalls all small boats.

POWDER.—Hoisted alone in port. Taking powder on board. Alone at sea. Distress.

RATING MARKS IN THE UNITED STATES NAVY.

THE INSIGNIA OF RANK OF COMMISSIONED, WARRANT, AND PETTY OFFICERS.

There are four classes of officers in the United States navy, and each has its own distinguishing mark.

The commissioned officers of the line.
The commissioned corps.
The warrant officers.
The petty officers.

The first two classes are graduates of Annapolis, or regularly commissioned by the Government. The last two are composed of enlisted men who have been promoted.

The rank device of the commissioned officers is worn on the shoulder-knot of the full dress uniform and on the collar of the service coat.

APPENDIX.

The marks are as follows:

REAR-ADMIRAL.

Foul anchor with silver stars at ends; and one stripe of gold lace two inches wide, and one of one-half inch wide above it, on sleeves.

COMMODORE.

A star with a foul anchor at either side of it; and one stripe of gold lace two inches wide on sleeves.

CAPTAIN.

A spread eagle with foul anchor at either side. Four one-half-inch stripes of gold lace on sleeves.

COMMANDER.

Foul anchor with silver oak leaves at ends. Three stripes of half-inch gold lace on sleeves.

LIEUTENANT-COMMANDER.—A silver foul anchor with a silver oak leaf at either end. Two stripes of half-inch gold lace with a quarter-inch stripe between.

LIEUTENANT.

Silver foul anchor with two silver bars at either side. Two stripes of gold lace one-half inch wide on sleeves.

LIEUTENANT—JUNIOR GRADE.

Silver foul anchor with one silver bar at either side. Two stripes of gold lace, half and quarter-inch, on sleeves.

ENSIGN.

A gold foul anchor on collar or shoulder-knot and one stripe of gold lace on sleeves.

THE COMMISSIONED CORPS.

The commissioned corps' devices are substituted for the anchor by staff officers, who wear the same rank devices as are prescribed for line officers with whom they have relative rank.

THE PAY CORPS.—A silver oak sprig and a narrow band of white cloth above and below the gold lace on sleeves.

THE MEDICAL CORPS.—A spread oak leaf of gold with an acorn of silver, and a band of dark maroon velvet above and below the gold lace on sleeves.

THE ENGINEER CORPS.—Four silver oak leaves, and a band of red cloth above and below the gold lace on sleeves.

PETTY OFFICERS' RATING MARKS.

All petty officers wear a rating device on the sleeve of the outer garment above the elbow. If they belong to the starboard watch the mark will be sewed on the right sleeve; if the port, on the left.

QUARTERMASTER.

The petty officers' device always has a spread eagle above it. The specialty mark indicating to which department he belongs is just below in the angle formed by the chevrons. The chevrons indicate the class. Three chevrons, first class; two, second class, and so on. The chief petty

APPENDIX.

officers have an arch of the same cloth connecting the two ends of the top chevron.

The specialty marks are as follows:

| MASTER-AT-ARMS. | GUNNER'S MATES. | SEAMAN GUNNER. | CHIEF YEOMAN. |

| APOTHECARY. | YEOMAN—1ST, 2D, AND 3D CLASS. | SHIP'S PRINTER OR SCHOOLMASTER. | BANDMASTER. |

| MACHINISTS, BOILER-MAKERS, WATER-TENDERS, COPPERSMITHS, AND OILERS. | CARPENTER'S MATES, PLUMBERS, AND PAINTERS. | BLACKSMITH. | BOATSWAIN'S MATES AND COXSWAINS. |

The seaman class is indicated by the rows of braid on the cuffs.

Seamen, first class or able-bodied seamen, have three rows of braid.

Seamen, second class or ordinary seamen, have two rows of braid.

Seamen, third class or landsmen, have one row of braid.

The watch mark for the enlisted men not petty officers consists of a stripe of braid on the sleeve close to the shoulder. For the seaman, white on blue clothes, blue on white clothes.

For the engineer force, red on both white and blue clothes.

The watch mark indicates the watch of which the wearer is a member. The starboard men wear it on the right arm, and the port men on the left.

TAKING SOUNDINGS.

HEAVING THE LEAD.

The man using the "lead line" (as the sounding-line weighted with lead is called) stands on a grating that projects over the side. This is placed near enough so that the steersman can hear the man who "heaves the lead" when he calls out the number of fathoms of water. This he tells by the marks on the "lead line" as follows:

2 fathoms, twelve feet, 2 strips of leather.
3 " 3 strips of leather.
5 " white rag.
7 " red rag.
10 " leather with hole in it.
13 " 3 strips of leather or blue rag.
15 " white rag.
17 " red rag.
20 " 2 knots.
25 " 1 knot.
30 " 3 knots.
35 " 1 knot.
40 " 4 knots.
9 " are called mark.
11 " " " deeps.

APPENDIX.

The leadsman stands on his little grating and swings the lead so it just clears the water. When it is swinging well he lets it fly in the direction in which the ship is moving and then notes the depth by the strips of leather or rags. The result is shouted out so the steersman can hear and keep the vessel in the channel.

THE BOATSWAIN'S CALLS.

The boatswain's calls or "pipes" are very difficult to reduce to a musical scale, because the pitch of the instrument depends entirely on the amount of energy expended by the blower. The novice, after a few trials, would probably assert that the primitive little whistle had only one note—and not very much of that ; but he would be surprised indeed at the volume of sound, the range, and the command over the instrument which a veteran boatswain would soon make everyday matter to him. Not only do these experts sound the regular calls with ear-piercing exactness, but actual tunes are often included in their repertoire.

The pipe or whistle is held with the bulb in the centre of the palm, the hole being towards the wrist. The lobe to which the ring and lanyard are attached, serves simply as a handle.

In the diagram given, the black line indicates the "pipe" or call ; the four faint horizontal lines, the notes, and the vertical bars, the time.

The roll indicated by the wavy line in the diagram is

made by rapidly opening and closing the hand. The gradual rise and fall is effected in the same way, but slowly. The rattle is done by a quick movement of the tongue.

This diagram is furnished by an old boatswain. As a rule, the calls are taught entirely by personal instruction, and it is believed that they have here been put into print for the first time. None of the ordinary manuals have ever given them, the young sailor having had to learn them by experience on shipboard.

Their importance is evident from the fact that every order aboard ship is preceded by the pipe peculiar to the command; for though the words may not be heard, the whistle can always be distinguished. Even the most lubberly landsman, with such continuous practice, soon learns the meaning of the different calls, and jumps to obey them.

THE BOATSWAIN'S CALLS

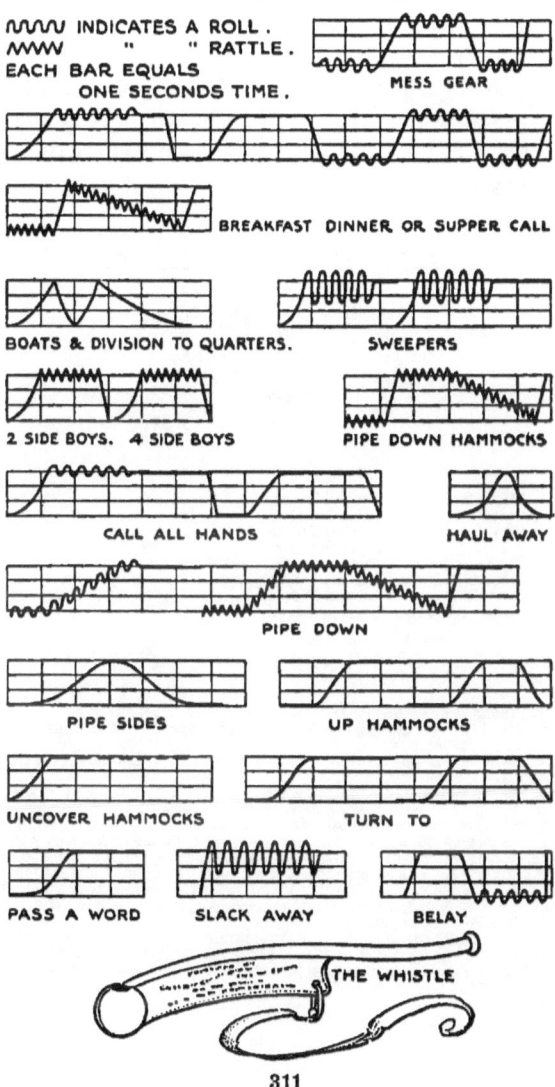

STATIONS OR QUARTERS FOR EXERCISE, OR PRECEDING ACTION, OF FIVE-INCH BREECHLOADING RIFLES.

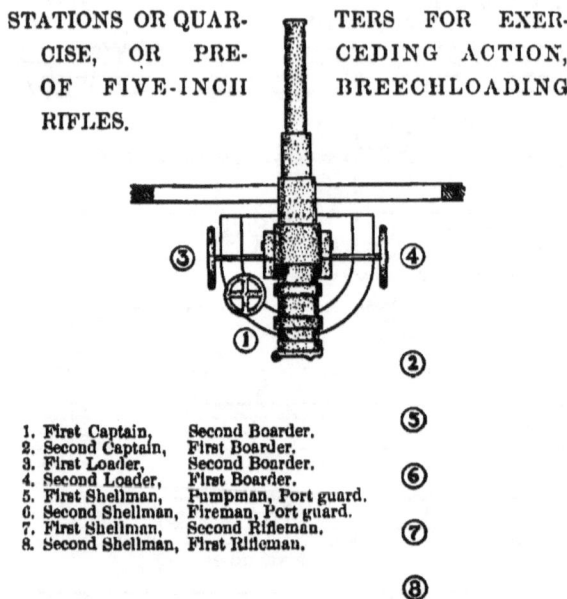

1. First Captain,   Second Boarder.
2. Second Captain,   First Boarder.
3. First Loader,   Second Boarder.
4. Second Loader,   First Boarder.
5. First Shellman,   Pumpman, Port guard.
6. Second Shellman,   Fireman, Port guard.
7. First Shellman,   Second Rifleman.
8. Second Shellman,   First Rifleman.

1. Stands at elevating gear wheel and sights and fires the gun.
2. Stands at the right and beside the breech; opens same after firing so shell can be taken out.
3. Stands at the left training wheel—*i.e.*, the wheel that moves the gun laterally. He also loads the gun.
4. Stands at the right training wheel. He takes out the empty shell after firing, and wears heavy gloves for that purpose.
5 and 6. Stand just behind No. 2 to the right of the gun. They may be termed emergency men. They assist with the shells, carry the wounded, if any; will be called away in case of fire, and are qualified to sight and fire the gun in case the first and second captains are wounded or killed. They provide revolvers and belts for Nos. 1, 2, and 3, and belts for Nos. 5, 6, 7, and 8. They are also port guards, and defend the ports in case of close action.
7 and 8. Carry shells from the ammunition hoist to a position amidships convenient for quick transport to the gun. They are also riflemen, and may be called to protect any part of the ship from boarders or from fire on shore.

www.ingramcontent.com/pod-product-compliance
Lightning Source LLC
Chambersburg PA
CBHW031417230426
43668CB00007B/337